Pass It On!

Ready-to-Use Handouts
for Asset Builders

Second Edition

Pass It On!

Ready-to-Use Handouts for Asset Builders, Second Edition

The following are registered trademarks of Search Institute: Search Institute®, Developmental Assets®, and Healthy Communities · Healthy Youth®.

Jolene Roehlkepartain
Copyright © 1999, 2006 by Search Institute

A Search Institute Publication

At the time of publication, all facts and figures cited herein are the most current available; all telephone numbers, addresses, and Web site URLs are accurate and active; all publications, organizations, Web sites, and other resources exist as described in this book; and all efforts have been made to verify them. The author and Search Institute make no warranty or guarantee concerning the information and materials given out by organizations or content found at Web sites that are cited herein, and we are not responsible for any changes that occur after this book's publication. If you find an error or believe that a resource listed herein is not as described, please contact Client Services at Search Institute.

10 9 8 7 6 5

Printed on acid-free paper in the United States of America.

Search Institute
615 First Avenue Northeast, Suite 125
Minneapolis, MN 55413
www.search-institute.org
612-376-8955 · 800-888-7828

ISBN-13: 978-1-57482-243-4
ISBN-10: 1-57482-243-8

Credits
Contributing Editor: Jolene Roehlkepartain
Editors: Jennifer Griffin-Wiesner, Claudia Hoffacker

Contributors: Carolyn "Tunie" Munson-Benson, Stephen L. Onell, Scott Richardson, Marilyn Peplau, and The Healthy Communities · Healthy Youth Team of New Richmond, Wisconsin.

Reviewers: Mary Ackerman, Karen Bartig, Nancy Tellet-Royce, Tenessa Gemelke, Bill Kauffmann, Terri Swanson.

Book Design: Nancy Johansen-Wester
Production Supervisor: Mary Ellen Buscher

Library of Congress Cataloging-in-Publication Data
Roehlkepartain, Jolene L., 1962-
  Pass it on! : ready-to-use handouts for asset builders / Jolene Roehlkepartain. — 2nd ed.
      p. cm.
  Summary: "From the bus driver to school nurse to grandparents to the manager at the corner store - everyone in a community has an impact on kids. Is it a positive impact or a negative one? This collection of easy-to-read reproducible handouts provides inspiration and practical suggestions for everyone in a community to support and encourage young people to be their very best"—Provided by publisher.
  ISBN-13: 978-1-57482-243-4 (pbk. : alk. paper)
  ISBN-10: 1-57482-243-8 (pbk. : alk. paper)
  1. Children—Conduct of life. 2. Children—Life skills guides. 3. Teenagers—Conduct of life.
4. Teenagers—Life skills guides. 5. Values. 6. Sucess. I. Title.
  BJ1631.R64 2006
  649'.1—dc22   2006016354

About Search Institute

Search Institute is an independent, nonprofit, nonsectarian organization whose mission is to provide leadership, knowledge, and resources to promote healthy children, youth, and communities. The institute collaborates with others to promote long-term organizational and cultural change that supports its mission. For a free information packet, call 800-888-7828.

About this Book

Since the launch of the Healthy Communities · Healthy Youth initiative in 1996, people all over the United States, Canada, and other countries have realized the power of assets to help kids succeed. As the asset-building movement grows, so does the need for specific information on what individuals and groups can do to build assets. That's what *Pass It On!* is for. In this book you will find asset-building tips and information for everyone from brothers and sisters to grandparents to police officers. There are handouts for groups and organizations as well.

We hope you will use these handouts often. They are designed to be quick, practical tools for easy distribution. You can make as many copies as you want and give them to as many people as you want. (See below for licensing and copyright information.) Use these sheets to help spread the word about asset building in your school, neighborhood, organization, community, and beyond.

More than 10,000 asset champions have used the first edition of *Pass It On!*, finding that it made the job of spreading the Developmental Assets message much easier. Since that first edition was published in 1999, Search Institute has conducted new research on Developmental Assets. *Pass It On!, Second Edition,* provides updated information based on data collected in 2010. You'll find new asset-building ideas and resources. In addition, we have included a set of popular handouts from our resource *Pass It On at School*, which is now out of print. These handouts provide concrete activities for teachers, counselors and school administrators to start building assets in their schools. All handouts are available as downloads at **www.search-institute.org/oc/passio.**

Licensing and Copyright

The handouts in *Pass It On! Ready-to-Use Handouts for Asset Builders, Second Edition,* may be copied from this book or printed from the handout files available as downloads, as many times for as many people as you want. For each copy, please respect the following guidelines:

- · Do not remove, alter, or obscure the Search Institute credit and copyright information on any handout.
- · Clearly differentiate any material you add for local distribution from material prepared by Search Institute.
- · Do not alter the Search Institute material in content or meaning.
- · Do not resell the handouts for profit.

Include the following attribution when you use the information from the handouts in other formats for promotional or educational purposes:

Printing Tips

These handouts will be more effective at getting the word out about asset building if the copies you distribute are neat and easy to read. Here are some things you can do to get high-quality reproduction without spending a lot of money.

- Always copy from the original in the book or from a copy printed from the handout files available as downloads. Copying from a copy lowers the reproduction quality.
- Store the originals in a safe place where they won't get bent or damaged.
- Make copies more appealing by using bright colored paper. Often a quick-print shop will have daily specials on certain colors of paper or ink.
- Consider printing each handout on a different color paper for variety.
- If you are using more than one handout or a handout that is more than one page, make two-sided copies.
- Make sure the paper weight is heavy enough (use at least 60-pound offset paper) so that the words don't bleed through (as often happens with 20-pound paper).

About the Contributors

Carolyn "Tunie" Munson-Benson is a parent, writer, educator, and children's literature specialist. She's the author of *Playful Reading*; director of the Early Bird Project, promoting early literacy; and founder of the Book Nook Program, a community-based celebration of children's literature in the schools.

Stephen L. Onell, M.S., L.I.S.W., is director of the Lakes Area Children, Youth & Family Services, including a program for fathers called Fathers First!, in Vadnais Heights, Minnesota. Besides his professional work in family and youth services, he is a parent, community volunteer, educator, social worker, consultant, and workshop trainer in asset building.

Scott Richardson is director of community relations for Northfield Hospital in Northfield, Minnesota. He is a board member for the Northfield Healthy Community Initiative. Mr. Richardson has contributed to the initiatives' marketing and communications work and contributed handouts in those areas.

Jolene Roehlkepartain is a writer, a parent, and the author of *Building Assets Together, Ideas for Parents* newsletter, and *Parenting Preschoolers with a Purpose*. She is also the co-author of *What Young Children Need to Succeed* and the author or co-author of 16 other books.

Marilyn Peplau is a Search Institute trainer and former guidance counselor for the New Richmond School District in New Richmond, Wisconsin. She was the team leader for the New Richmond Healthy Communities · Healthy Youth initiative and coordinated the creative efforts of the group for the first edition of *Pass it On!*

In addition, much of the information in these handouts is based on Search Institute's experience in working with hundreds of community and statewide asset-building initiatives.

Contents

Part 6 Spanish Handouts (Handouts 79-89)

Part 7 The List of Developmental Assets in French (Handout 90)

Grouping Handouts for Specific Sectors

It is a good idea to always include the list(s) of assets and introductory handouts, along with other helpful handouts you distribute. It gives people the context for the ideas. In addition, handouts can be grouped together for specific audiences. Here are some suggestions:

Families

20. Asset-Building Ideas for Young People
21. Asset-Building Ideas for Children
22. Asset-Building Ideas for Parents and Guardians
23. Asset-Building Ideas for Grandparents
24. Asset-Building Ideas for Brothers and Sisters
25. Asset-Building Ideas for Neighbors and Neighborhood Groups
67. Asset-Building Resources for Parents and Guardians
70. Reading Tips for Infants and Toddlers (Ages Birth to 2)
71. Reading Tips for Children Ages 3 to 5
72. Reading Tips for Children Ages 5 to 9
73. Reading Tips for Children Ages 9 to 12
74. Reading Tips for Young People Ages 12 to 18
76. Finding Asset-Building Books for Kids
77. Web Sites with Asset-Building Themes

Children and Young People

7. 40 Developmental Assets for Early Childhood (Ages 3 to 5)—chart
8. 40 Developmental Assets for Middle Childhood (Ages 8 to 12)—chart
9. 40 Developmental Assets for Adolescents (Ages 12 to 18)—chart
20. Asset-Building Ideas for Young People
21. Asset-Building Ideas for Children
24. Asset-Building Ideas for Brothers and Sisters
25. Asset-Building Ideas for Neighbors and Neighborhood Groups
26. Asset-Building Ideas for Babysitters
78. Asset-Building Ideas for Choosing and Talking about Movies and TV Shows

Pass It On!

Children-, Youth-, and Family-Serving Organizations

Government Agencies

Faith-Based Organizations

Pass It On!

Corporate and Philanthropic Foundations

Healthy Communites • Healthy Youth Initiatives

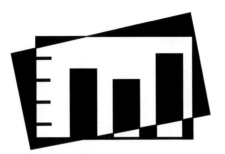

Part 1

Introducing Developmental Assets

Handouts 1-9

What Are
Developmental **Assets?**

Do you ever wonder why some kids seem to grow up with ease while others struggle? Are you surprised that some kids thrive in spite of difficult circumstances?

Search Institute is a nonprofit research organization in Minneapolis, Minnesota, that has been asking these same questions since 1958. Through studies involving hundreds of thousands of young people across the country, Search Institute has found 40 factors that are essential to young people's success. They call these 40 factors Developmental Assets. These assets aren't financial. Instead, they are opportunities, skills, relationships, values, and self-perceptions that all young people need in their lives.

The assets are both external (things that other people provide for youth) and internal (things that young people develop within themselves). There are four categories of external assets and four categories of internal assets.

EXTERNAL ASSETS

Support
Young people need to be supported, cared for, and loved by their families and many others. They also need organizations and institutions, such as schools and faith-based organizations, that provide positive, supportive environments. There are six Support assets:

Asset 1— Family Support
Asset 2— Positive Family Communication
Asset 3— Other Adult Relationships
Asset 4— Caring Neighborhood
Asset 5— Caring School Climate
Asset 6— Parent Involvement in Schooling

Empowerment
Young people need to feel that their community values them and that they have important ways to contribute. They must also feel safe. There are four Empowerment assets:

Asset 7— Community Values Youth
Asset 8— Youth as Resources
Asset 9— Service to Others
Asset 10— Safety

Boundaries and Expectations
Young people need to know what is expected of them and whether activities and behaviors are acceptable or not acceptable. There are six Boundaries-and-Expectations assets:

Asset 11— Family Boundaries
Asset 12— School Boundaries
Asset 13— Neighborhood Boundaries
Asset 14— Adult Role Models
Asset 15— Positive Peer Influence
Asset 16— High Expectations

Constructive Use of Time

Young people need to spend their time in positive, healthy ways. This includes doing activities in youth programs, in faith-based institutions, and at home. There are four Constructive-Use-of-Time assets:

Asset 17— Creative Activities
Asset 18— Youth Programs
Asset 19— Religious Community
Asset 20— Time at Home

INTERNAL ASSETS

Commitment to Learning

Young people do best when they develop a strong interest in and commitment to education and learning. There are five Commitment-to-Learning assets:

Asset 21— Achievement Motivation
Asset 22— School Engagement
Asset 23— Homework
Asset 24— Bonding to School
Asset 25— Reading for Pleasure

Positive Values

Young people thrive when they develop strong values that guide their choices. There are six Positive-Values assets:

Asset 26— Caring
Asset 27— Equality and Social Justice
Asset 28— Integrity
Asset 29— Honesty
Asset 30— Responsibility
Asset 31— Restraint

Social Competencies

Young people benefit from having skills and competencies that equip them to make positive choices, to build relationships, and to deal with difficult situations. Five assets make up the category of Social Competencies:

Asset 32— Planning and Decision Making
Asset 33— Interpersonal Competence
Asset 34— Cultural Competence
Asset 35— Resistance Skills
Asset 36— Peaceful Conflict Resolution

Positive Identity

Young people need to develop a strong sense of their own power, purpose, worth, and promise. There are four Positive-Identity assets:

Asset 37— Personal Power
Asset 38— Self-Esteem
Asset 39— Sense of Purpose
Asset 40— Positive View of Personal Future

The Power of
Developmental **Assets**

THE POWER OF ASSETS TO PROMOTE
POSITIVE ATTITUDES AND BEHAVIORS*

Having more Developmental Assets increases the chances that young people will have positive attitudes and behaviors. Search Institute research has found that young people with more assets are more likely to participate in eight positive behaviors. Here are some examples:

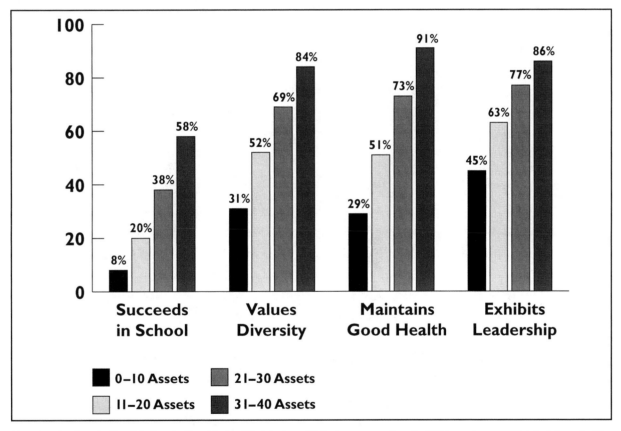

*Based on data from the *Search Institute Profiles of Student Life: Attitudes and Behaviors* survey; gathered in 2010 from almost 90,000 students in grades 6 to 12 (ages approximately 11 to 18) from 111 communities in 26 U.S. states.

THE POWER OF ASSETS TO PROTECT*

Assets can help protect young people from making many harmful and unhealthy choices. Youth with more assets are less likely than youth with fewer assets to engage in 24 risky behaviors, such as tobacco use, gambling, violence, and shoplifting. This chart shows this relationship:

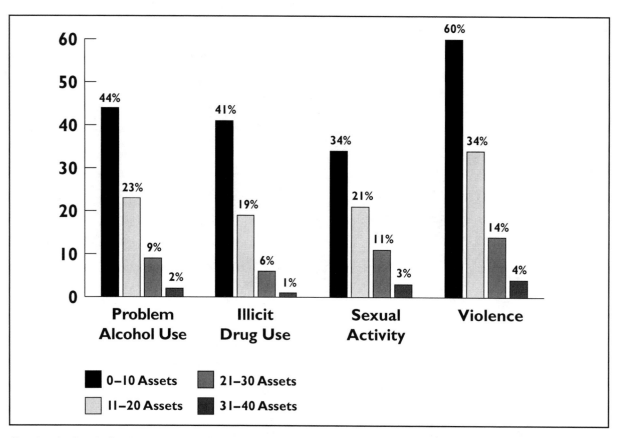

*Based on data from the *Search Institute Profiles of Student Life: Attitudes and Behaviors* survey; gathered in 2010 from almost 90,000 students in grades 6 to 12 (ages approximately 11 to 18) from 111 communities in 26 U.S. states.

Fast Facts about
Developmental Assets for Young People*

Immunizations keep young children healthy and protect them from disease. Similarly, Developmental Assets help kids make healthy choices and inoculate them against a wide range of risk-taking behaviors, including substance abuse, violence, and school failure. The more assets young people have, the more likely they are to be healthy.

Most young people surveyed by Search Institute have at least some assets (83 percent say they have 11 or more). But having only some of the assets is like getting only some of your shots. You might be protected against measles, but you could still get polio or hepatitis. That's why it's important to focus on giving young people all of the assets they need to be healthy.

Other facts about Developmental Assets:

• **Young people with more assets are less likely to engage in risk-taking behaviors.** Young people with 10 or fewer assets say they are involved in an average of about 3.8 high-risk behaviors. Young people with 31 assets or more report an average of less than 1 high-risk behavior.

• **As young people's assets increase, their positive behaviors also increase.** While young people with 10 or fewer assets report an average of 2.6 positive behaviors, those with 31 assets or more average 6.2 positive behaviors. This includes succeeding in school, helping others, valuing diversity, and exhibiting leadership.

• **The average young person surveyed has 20 of the 40 assets.** But levels of assets decrease for older youth. While the average student in grade six surveyed has 22.7 assets, the average student in grade 12 surveyed has 19 assets.

• **The most common is asset 40: Positive View of Personal Future.** Seventy-five percent of young people surveyed report having this asset.

• **The least common is asset 17: Creative Activities.** Only 20 percent of young people report having this asset.

• **Girls, on average, have more assets than boys.** However, boys are more likely to have assets 10: Safety; 38: Self-Esteem; and 39: Sense of Purpose.

• **Most assets decrease in frequency between grades 6 and 12. The assets that decrease the most are** 12: School Boundaries (74 percent vs. 44 percent); 15: Positive Peer Influence (87 percent vs. 50 percent); and 31: Restraint (73 percent of grade 6 students vs. 21 percent of grade 12 students).

• **Assets that increase in frequency between grades 6 and 12 are** 10: Safety (41 percent vs. 68 percent); 23: Homework (33 percent vs. 50 percent); and 37: Personal Power (39 percent vs. 54 percent).

*Based on data from the *Search Institute Profiles of Student Life: Attitudes and Behaviors* survey; gathered in 2010 from almost 90,000 students in grades 6 to 12 (ages approximately 11 to 18) from 111 communities in 26 U.S. states.

THE GAP IN ASSETS AMONG YOUNG PEOPLE*

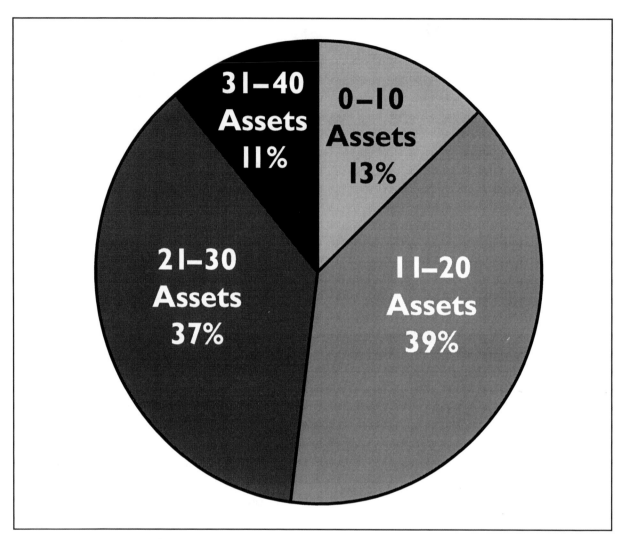

*Based on data from the *Search Institute Profiles of Student Life: Attitudes and Behaviors* survey; gathered in 2010 from almost 90,000 students in grades 6 to 12 (ages approximately 11 to 18) from 111 communities in 26 U.S. states.

Frequently Asked Questions
about the Asset Framework

Search Institute has found that some questions about the asset framework come up again and again. Here are answers to a number of them:

1. I don't have kids, and I don't work with kids—can I build assets?

Yes! One of the most important messages of asset building is that everyone plays a role, not just families, youth workers, and teachers. The assets offer ways everyone can provide the positive relationships and experiences young people need. For some, it may be as simple as smiling and saying hello to young people encountered during daily activities. For others, it could mean developing a significant relationship with a young person. Even using the asset framework to assess candidates for public office can be a way of supporting asset building.

2. Are resources on the assets available in any other language?

Yes. Search Institute has several resources in Spanish, including the list of 40 assets. This list is also available in French. When distributing the list, consider using English on one side and Spanish or French on the other, depending on the languages spoken in your area.

3. Do younger children need the same assets as teenagers?

The Developmental Assets framework applies to all ages. The core of each asset is important to children of all ages but experienced, built, and defined differently at different stages of development. Search Institute has developed frameworks for early childhood (ages 3 to 5), middle childhood (ages 8 to 12), and adolescents (ages 12 to 18), and researchers continue to work on defining the assets for children of all ages.

4. How important is it that I focus on each individual asset?

While each individual asset is critical to development, it's more important (and easier!) to pay attention to the eight categories of assets and the broader concepts of external assets and internal assets.

5. What's the best way to develop an understanding of the assets?

Share your ideas, questions, suggestions, stories, and frustrations with others. Talk about how the 40 assets work in your own experience, and how they connect to your own values and ideals.

6. Once a young person has a particular asset, does he or she have it forever?

No. Assets can come and go, based on current relationships and experiences. They need to be built throughout a person's life.

7. Is it important for asset-building initiatives to find ways to exemplify the asset focus in our structure, meetings, and planning?

Yes! This is a great way to reinforce people's understanding of the assets, and it can also lead to stronger teams and organizations. For example, some organizations use the eight categories of assets to look at how they work together, asking questions like: How can we support each other? What should be our boundaries and expectations for meetings? and so on.

8. Are some assets more important than others?

Don't pick and choose assets—the power of this framework lies in how they work together. Young people need as many of the assets as they can get. If you want to focus specific attention on one or two assets at a time, do so with the reminder that they are only part of the larger framework.

9. Is it OK to focus on just the assets that seem most critical for our kids?

Yes. You can use the asset framework to help set priorities in your community. For example, some communities have looked at the framework and realized they haven't done much to address issues of boundaries. Others have found that there are few opportunities for young people to be involved in constructive activities.

10. A lot of activities are "asset building," but few people have heard of the concept. How can we get other "asset builders" on board?

Celebrate, affirm, and honor the ways people already build assets (even if they don't call it that). A good way to first get people excited is to have them go through the list and mark what they're already doing. People and organizations that build assets can also be acknowledged and featured in your community newspaper or other public forum.

11. Does having more assets just reduce risk-taking behaviors?

No. The assets also promote positive outcomes and positive behavior, such as academic success, leadership skills, and healthy lifestyle.

12. Do we have to create a new program based on asset building?

No. You can use the asset framework to help evaluate and improve existing programs and opportunities for young people. For example: How can a focus on assets improve meetings? How can it enhance what's happening in a 4-H group? How can it impact a community-wide celebration?

13. Can a single action help to build more than one of the assets?

Certainly! For example, a caring relationship with an adult (asset 3) can lead to many of the other assets, including Community Values Youth (asset 7), Adult Role Models (asset 14), and Self-Esteem (asset 38).

Principles of **Asset Building**

On average, young people surveyed by Search Institute experience only about 19 of the 40 assets. Thus, a commitment to asset building should become a top priority for every individual, every organization, and every community. Search Institute has identified six principles that can help shape our asset-building efforts:

☞ All children and young people need assets.

Research shows that all young people, regardless of gender, age, family composition, race, or ethnicity, can benefit from having more assets. While we must continue to pay special attention to children and young people who are in crisis and high-risk situations, the central challenge is to generate the kind of attention that will help *all* young people.

☞ Relationships are key.

Building assets calls upon every single person to build both formal and informal relationships with young people that are positive and caring.

☞ Everyone can build assets.

In an asset-building community, everyone works at developing caring relationships with young people.

☞ Building assets is an ongoing process.

Asset building begins before birth or adoption, by equipping parents-to-be with skills and knowledge to care for a baby or child. And asset building continues throughout childhood and adolescence and into adulthood. Young people need their assets nurtured every day during every year of their childhood and adolescence.

☞ Asset building requires consistent messages.

For asset building to be woven into the fabric of community life, it needs to be reinforced everywhere. That means in homes, schools, congregations, places of employment, clubs. Everywhere.

☞ Duplication and repetition are good and important.

Young people need as many asset-building experiences as possible.

The **Asset-Building** **Difference**

For healthy development to occur for all children and youth, we need to rebuild communities where people and organizations feel connected, engaged, responsible, and committed to young people. In order to do this, some essential shifts in thinking need to happen.

MOVING FROM...	TO...
Talking about problems	Talking about positives and possibilities
Focusing on troubled and troubling youth	Focusing on all children and adolescents
Focusing primarily on ages birth to 5	Focusing on all young people, ages birth to 18
Age segregation	Intergenerational community
Viewing young people as problems	Seeing youth as resources
Reacting to problems	Being proactive about building strengths
Blaming others	Claiming personal responsibility
Treating youth as objects of programs	Respecting youth as actors in their own development
Relying on professionals	Involving everyone in the lives of young people
Competing priorities	Cooperative efforts
Conflicting signals about values and priorities	Consistent messages about what is important
Managing crises	Building a shared vision
Despair	Hope

40 Developmental Assets
for Early Childhood (Ages 3 to 5)

Search Institute has identified the following building blocks of development that help young children ages 3 to 5 grow up healthy, caring, and responsible.

CATEGORY	ASSET NAME AND DEFINITION
Support	1. **Family Support**—Parent(s) and/or primary caregiver(s) provide the child with high levels of consistent and predictable love, physical care, and positive attention in ways that are responsive to the child's individuality. 2. **Positive Family Communication**—Parent(s) and/or primary caregiver(s) express themselves positively and respectfully, engaging young children in conversations that invite their input. 3. **Other Adult Relationships**—With the family's support, the child experiences consistent, caring relationships with adults outside the family. 4. **Caring Neighbors**—The child's network of relationships includes neighbors who provide emotional support and a sense of belonging. 5. **Caring Climate in Child-Care and Educational Settings**—Caregivers and teachers create environments that are nurturing, accepting, encouraging, and secure. 6. **Parent Involvement in Child Care and Education**—Parent(s), caregivers, and teachers together create a consistent and supportive approach to fostering the child's successful growth.
Empowerment	7. **Community Cherishes and Values Young Children**—Children are welcomed and included throughout community life. 8. **Children Seen as Resources**—The community demonstrates that children are valuable resources by investing in a child-rearing system of family support and high-quality activities and resources to meet children's physical, social, and emotional needs. 9. **Service to Others**—The child has opportunities to perform simple but meaningful and caring actions for others. 10. **Safety**—Parent(s), caregivers, teachers, neighbors, and the community take action to ensure children's health and safety.
Boundaries and Expectations	11. **Family Boundaries**—The family provides consistent supervision for the child and maintains reasonable guidelines for behavior that the child can understand and achieve. 12. **Boundaries in Child-Care and Educational Settings**—Caregivers and educators use positive approaches to discipline and natural consequences to encourage self-regulation and acceptable behaviors. 13. **Neighborhood Boundaries**—Neighbors encourage the child in positive, acceptable behavior, as well as intervene in negative behavior, in a supportive, nonthreatening way. 14. **Adult Role Models**—Parent(s), caregivers, and other adults model self-control, social skills, engagement in learning, and healthy lifestyles. 15. **Positive Peer Relationships**—Parent(s) and caregivers seek to provide opportunities for the child to interact positively with other children. 16. **Positive Expectations**—Parent(s), caregivers, and teachers encourage and support the child in behaving appropriately, undertaking challenging tasks, and performing activities to the best of her or his abilities.
Constructive Use of Time	17. **Play and Creative Activities**—The child has daily opportunities to play in ways that allow self-expression, physical activity, and interaction with others. 18. **Out-of-Home and Community Programs**—The child experiences well-designed programs led by competent, caring adults in well-maintained settings. 19. **Religious Community**—The child participates in age-appropriate religious activities and caring relationships that nurture her or his spiritual development. 20. **Time at Home**—The child spends most of her or his time at home participating in family activities and playing constructively, with parent(s) guiding TV and electronic game use.

EXTERNAL ASSETS

CATEGORY	ASSET NAME AND DEFINITION
Commitment to Learning	**21. Motivation to Mastery**—The child responds to new experiences with curiosity and energy, resulting in the pleasure of mastering new learning and skills. **22. Engagement in Learning Experiences**—The child fully participates in a variety of activities that offer opportunities for learning. **23. Home–Program Connection**—The child experiences security, consistency, and connections between home and out-of-home care programs and learning activities. **24. Bonding to Programs**—The child forms meaningful connections with out-of-home care and educational programs. **25. Early Literacy**—The child enjoys a variety of pre-reading activities, including adults reading to her or him daily, looking at and handling books, playing with a variety of media, and showing interest in pictures, letters, and numbers.
Positive Values	**26. Caring**—The child begins to show empathy, understanding, and awareness of others' feelings. **27. Equality and Social Justice**—The child begins to show concern for people who are excluded from play and other activities or not treated fairly because they are different. **28. Integrity**—The child begins to express her or his views appropriately and to stand up for a growing sense of what is fair and right. **29. Honesty**—The child begins to understand the difference between truth and lies, and is truthful to the extent of her or his understanding. **30. Responsibility**—The child begins to follow through on simple tasks to take care of her- or himself and to help others. **31. Self-Regulation**—The child increasingly can identify, regulate, and control her or his behaviors in healthy ways, using adult support constructively in particularly stressful situations.
Social Competencies	**32. Planning and Decision Making**—The child begins to plan for the immediate future, choosing from among several options and trying to solve problems. **33. Interpersonal Skills**—The child cooperates, shares, plays harmoniously, and comforts others in distress. **34. Cultural Awareness and Sensitivity**—The child begins to learn about her or his own cultural identity and to show acceptance of people who are racially, physically, culturally, or ethnically different from her or him. **35. Resistance Skills**—The child begins to sense danger accurately, to seek help from trusted adults, and to resist pressure from peers to participate in unacceptable or risky behavior. **36. Peaceful Conflict Resolution**—The child begins to compromise and resolve conflicts without using physical aggression or hurtful language.
Positive Identity	**37. Personal Power**—The child can make choices that give a sense of having some influence over things that happen in her or his life. **38. Self-Esteem**—The child likes her- or himself and has a growing sense of being valued by others. **39. Sense of Purpose**—The child anticipates new opportunities, experiences, and milestones in growing up. **40. Positive View of Personal Future**—The child finds the world interesting and enjoyable, and feels that he or she has a positive place in it.

INTERNAL ASSETS

40 Developmental Assets
for Middle Childhood (Ages 8 to 12)

Search Institute has identified the following building blocks of development that help children ages 8 to 12 grow up healthy, caring, and responsible.

EXTERNAL ASSETS

CATEGORY	ASSET NAME AND DEFINITION
Support	1. **Family Support**—Family life provides high levels of love and support.
	2. **Positive Family Communication**—Parent(s) and child communicate positively. Child feels comfortable seeking advice and counsel from parent(s).
	3. **Other Adult Relationships**—Child receives support from adults other than her or his parent(s).
	4. **Caring Neighborhood**—Child experiences caring neighbors.
	5. **Caring School Climate**—Relationships with teachers and peers provide a caring, encouraging school environment.
	6. **Parent Involvement in Schooling**—Parent(s) are actively involved in helping the child succeed in school.
Empowerment	7. **Community Values Children**—Child feels valued and appreciated by adults in the community.
	8. **Children as Resources**—Child is included in decisions at home and in the community.
	9. **Service to Others**—Child has opportunities to help others in the community.
	10. **Safety**—Child feels safe at home, at school, and in her or his neighborhood.
Boundaries and Expectations	11. **Family Boundaries**—Family has clear and consistent rules and consequences and monitors the child's whereabouts.
	12. **School Boundaries**—School provides clear rules and consequences.
	13. **Neighborhood Boundaries**—Neighbors take responsibility for monitoring the child's behavior.
	14. **Adult Role Models**—Parent(s) and other adults in the child's family, as well as nonfamily adults, model positive, responsible behavior.
	15. **Positive Peer Influence**—Child's closest friends model positive, responsible behavior.
	16. **High Expectations**—Parent(s) and teachers expect the child to do her or his best at school and in other activities.
Constructive Use of Time	17. **Creative Activities**—Child participates in music, art, drama, or creative writing two or more times per week.
	18. **Child Programs**—Child participates two or more times per week in cocurricular school activities or structured community programs for children.
	19. **Religious Community**—Child attends religious programs or services one or more times per week.
	20. **Time at Home**—Child spends some time most days both in high-quality interaction with parents and doing things at home other than watching TV or playing video games.

CATEGORY	ASSET NAME AND DEFINITION
Commitment to Learning	**21. Achievement Motivation**—Child is motivated and strives to do well in school.
	22. Learning Engagement—Child is responsive, attentive, and actively engaged in learning at school and enjoys participating in learning activities outside of school.
	23. Homework—Child usually hands in homework on time.
	24. Bonding to Adults at School—Child cares about teachers and other adults at school.
	25. Reading for Pleasure—Child enjoys and engages in reading for fun most days of the week.
Positive Values	**26. Caring**—Parent(s) tell the child it is important to help other people.
	27. Equality and Social Justice—Parent(s) tell the child it is important to speak up for equal rights for all people.
	28. Integrity—Parent(s) tell the child it is important to stand up for one's beliefs.
	29. Honesty—Parent(s) tell the child it is important to tell the truth.
	30. Responsibility—Parent(s) tell the child it is important to accept personal responsibility for behavior.
	31. Healthy Lifestyle—Parent(s) tell the child it is important to have good health habits and an understanding of healthy sexuality.
Social Competencies	**32. Planning and Decision Making**—Child thinks about decisions and is usually happy with results of her or his decisions.
	33. Interpersonal Competence—Child cares about and is affected by other people's feelings, enjoys making friends, and, when frustrated or angry, tries to calm her- or himself.
	34. Cultural Competence—Child knows and is comfortable with people of different racial, ethnic, and cultural backgrounds and with her or his own cultural identity.
	35. Resistance Skills—Child can stay away from people who are likely to get her or him in trouble and is able to say no to doing wrong or dangerous things.
	36. Peaceful Conflict Resolution—Child attempts to resolve conflict nonviolently.
Positive Identity	**37. Personal Power**—Child feels he or she has some influence over things that happen in her or his life.
	38. Self-Esteem—Child likes and is proud to be the person he or she is.
	39. Sense of Purpose—Child sometimes thinks about what life means and whether there is a purpose for her or his life.
	40. Positive View of Personal Future—Child is optimistic about her or his personal future.

INTERNAL ASSETS

40 Developmental Assets
for Adolescents (Ages 12 to 18)

Search Institute has identified the following building blocks of development that help young people (ages 12 to 18) grow up healthy, caring, and responsible.

CATEGORY	ASSET NAME AND DEFINITION
Support	1. **Family Support**—Family life provides high levels of love and support.
	2. **Positive Family Communication**—Young person and her or his parent(s) communicate positively, and young person is willing to seek advice and counsel from parent(s).
	3. **Other Adult Relationships**—Young person receives support from three or more non-parent adults.
	4. **Caring Neighborhood**—Young person experiences caring neighbors.
	5. **Caring School Climate**—School provides a caring, encouraging environment.
	6. **Parent Involvement in Schooling**—Parent(s) are actively involved in helping young person succeed in school.
Empowerment	7. **Community Values Youth**—Young person perceives that adults in the community value youth.
	8. **Youth as Resources**—Young people are given useful roles in the community.
	9. **Service to Others**—Young person serves in the community one hour or more per week.
	10. **Safety**—Young person feels safe at home, school, and in the neighborhood.
Boundaries and Expectations	11. **Family Boundaries**—Family has clear rules and consequences and monitors the young person's whereabouts.
	12. **School Boundaries**—School provides clear rules and consequences.
	13. **Neighborhood Boundaries**—Neighbors take responsibility for monitoring young people's behavior.
	14. **Adult Role Models**—Parent(s) and other adults model positive, responsible behavior.
	15. **Positive Peer Influence**—Young person's best friends model responsible behavior.
	16. **High Expectations**—Both parent(s) and teachers encourage the young person to do well.
Constructive Use of Time	17. **Creative Activities**—Young person spends three or more hours per week in lessons or practice in music, theater, or other arts.
	18. **Youth Programs**—Young person spends three or more hours per week in sports, clubs, or organizations at school and/or in the community.
	19. **Religious Community**—Young person spends one or more hours per week in activities in a religious institution.
	20. **Time at Home**—Young person is out with friends "with nothing special to do" two or fewer nights per week.

EXTERNAL ASSETS

CATEGORY	ASSET NAME AND DEFINITION
Commitment to Learning	21. **Achievement Motivation**—Young person is motivated to do well in school.
	22. **School Engagement**—Young person is actively engaged in learning.
	23. **Homework**—Young person reports doing at least one hour of homework every school day.
	24. **Bonding to School**—Young person cares about her or his school.
	25. **Reading for Pleasure**—Young person reads for pleasure three or more hours per week.
Positive Values	26. **Caring**—Young person places high value on helping other people.
	27. **Equality and Social Justice**—Young person places high value on promoting equality and reducing hunger and poverty.
	28. **Integrity**—Young person acts on convictions and stands up for her or his beliefs.
	29. **Honesty**—Young person "tells the truth even when it is not easy."
	30. **Responsibility**—Young person accepts and takes personal responsibility.
	31. **Restraint**—Young person believes it is important not to be sexually active or to use alcohol or other drugs.
Social Competencies	32. **Planning and Decision Making**—Young person knows how to plan ahead and make choices.
	33. **Interpersonal Competence**—Young person has empathy, sensitivity, and friendship skills.
	34. **Cultural Competence**—Young person has knowledge of and comfort with people of different cultural/racial/ethnic backgrounds.
	35. **Resistance Skills**—Young person can resist negative peer pressure and dangerous situations.
	36. **Peaceful Conflict Resolution**—Young person seeks to resolve conflict nonviolently.
Positive Identity	37. **Personal Power**—Young person feels he or she has control over "things that happen to me."
	38. **Self-Esteem**—Young person reports having a high self-esteem.
	39. **Sense of Purpose**—Young person reports that "my life has a purpose."
	40. **Positive View of Personal Future**—Young person is optimistic about her or his personal future.

INTERNAL ASSETS

Part 2

Asset-Building Ideas for Individuals and Groups
Handouts 10-42

Building the **Support Assets**

All young people—no matter what their age—need support from caring and loving people. Here are ideas on how to build the six Support assets for children and youth as they grow up:

Ages Birth to 1	• Smile at every infant you see. • Spend as much time as possible holding babies and interacting with them.
Ages 1 to 2	• Say "yes" to children more often than "no." • Cheer children on as they master new skills. Comfort and guide them when they become frustrated.
Ages 3 to 5	• Get down to children's eye level whenever you interact with them. • Encourage children's thinking abilities by taking them to new places, such as a bird sanctuary, a candy manufacturer, or a concert designed for young children. Let them experience the sounds, sights, tastes, textures, and smells. • Play with children, letting them choose the activity.
Ages 6 to 11	• Encourage children's passions and interests. • Answer children's questions. If you don't know the answer, admit it and work together to find it. • When you and a child disagree, show you still care, and encourage other adults to do the same.
Ages 12 to 15	• Be available to listen. • Affirm independence and interdependence. People need each other.
Ages 16 to 18	• Find out what teenagers care about and advocate for their causes. • Ask teenagers for their opinion or advice. • Continue to show affection to teenagers by spending time with them—even if you're not doing or talking about anything special.

Pass It On!

Handout II

Building the
Empowerment Assets

All young people need to be empowered. In other words, they need to feel valued and valuable. Here are ideas on how to build the four Empowerment assets for children and youth at different ages:

Ages Birth to 1	• Realize that babies don't manipulate adults; respond immediately to their cries and needs. • Prop up babies and hold them so they can see more.
Ages 1 to 2	• Ensure safety by childproofing all environments where children play. If you're not sure what to do, ask your doctor, day-care provider, or early childhood educator. • Start introducing the value of community service by having children do simple tasks at home, such as putting a toy away in a toy box or picking up socks.
Ages 3 to 5	• Allow children to make simple choices, such as wearing a black shirt or a red shirt. • Teach children basic safety rules, such as never touching poisons and always wearing safety belts in the car. • Do simple acts of community service together with children such as collecting food for a food bank.
Ages 6 to 11	• Encourage children to write letters to the editor of your local paper about issues that are important to them. • Ask children what they like and do not like about their daily routines. Make changes to improve them.
Ages 12 to 15	• Encourage young people to volunteer at least one hour a week. Talk with them about what they learn from these experiences. • Talk with young people about their feelings and fears about safety. Work together to help young people feel more safe.
Ages 16 to 18	• Help teenagers spend time contributing to their communities. This could range from finding out about opportunities and how to get involved to simply figuring out ways to get them there. • Encourage teenagers to take leadership roles in addressing issues that concern them.

Building the **Boundaries-and-Expectations Assets**

All young people need to know their limits as well as what's expected of them. Here are ideas on how to build the six Boundaries-and-Expectations assets for children and youth at different ages:

Ages Birth to 1	• Realize that babies don't intentionally violate standards and boundaries. Don't punish them for violating boundaries they can't understand. • Distract children from inappropriate behavior and draw attention to how you want them to act.
Ages 1 to 2	• Give simple, understandable boundaries, such as, "Sit down," or "Don't bite." • Enforce boundaries consistently so children don't get confused. • Affirm children when they act appropriately.
Ages 3 to 5	• Stay calm when children act out in highly emotional ways. • Model how you want children to act; don't just tell them what to do and what not to do. • Learn what to expect from preschoolers. Read about child development in books and magazines, talk to other parents, or talk to preschool teachers or child-care workers.
Ages 6 to 11	• Encourage schools, neighbors, organizations, and communities to have consistent boundaries and consequences so children know how to act in different settings. • Be firm about boundaries that keep kids safe. Don't negotiate these boundaries. • Challenge children to do their best in school, and help them whenever you can.
Ages 12 to 15	• Be patient, calm, and consistent as young teenagers test the boundaries you set. • Negotiate new boundaries as children grow older. Work together on what's acceptable and what's not. • Ask young people where they are going and who they will be with.
Ages 16 to 18	• Help teenagers think about their goals for the future and what kind of boundaries they'll need to meet them. • Continue to have boundaries for appropriate behaviors and consequences for violating those boundaries. • Respect teenagers' privacy needs while showing interest in their friends and activities. • Challenge teenagers to do their best in school and other activities.

Building the Constructive-
Use-of-Time Assets

All children and youth need opportunities to be involved in positive, constructive activities. Here are ideas on how to build the four Constructive-Use-of-Time assets for children and youth at different ages:

Ages Birth to 1	• Be flexible with infant schedules, and gradually introduce predictable routines as babies get older. • Have babies spend most of their time with their parents or consistent caregivers.
Ages 1 to 2	• Balance stimulating, structured time with free playtime. • Have consistent times for children to sleep, eat, play, and relax.
Ages 3 to 5	• Take children to museums, theaters, and other cultural events or activities to expose them to new things. • Follow children's lead in which activities interest them.
Ages 6 to 11	• Allow children to have one or two regular out-of-home activities that are led by caring adults. • Teach children to balance their time so they gradually learn how to avoid getting too busy or too bored. • Volunteer in programs and activities for children, such as sports, clubs, religious activities, music, or others.
Ages 12 to 15	• Have a regular family night to do something fun together, and encourage others to do the same. • Help young people look for positive, stimulating activities that match their talents, interests, and abilities.
Ages 16 to 18	• Encourage teenagers to be involved in at least one activity that may continue into their adult years. • Help teenagers think about how the time they spend on different activities helps or hinders them in reaching their goals. • Volunteer in programs or activities for older teenagers. Take time to get to know the young people involved.

Pass It On!

Handout 14

Building the Commitment-to-Learning Assets

It is important for young people of all ages to value and have a commitment to lifelong learning. Here are ideas on how to build the five Commitment-to-Learning assets for children and youth at different ages:

Ages Birth to 1	• Give babies new, interesting things to look at, such as toys and books in different colors, shapes, and sizes. • Sing and read to babies every day.
Ages 1 to 2	• Take toddlers to new places, such as parks and stores. • Make up a game or song for children that teaches them the names of objects.
Ages 3 to 5	• Talk about what you see whenever you are with children and ask them to talk about what they see. • Visit libraries, zoos, museums—any places that give children new experiences.
Ages 6 to 11	• Set daily homework guidelines for children and provide a place for them to study. • Let children read to you every day as they learn to read. Show them that you are excited and proud about their reading. • Help children find ways to learn more about subjects that really interest them.
Ages 12 to 15	• Find creative ways to help young people link their interests with school subjects (such as doing special projects). • Encourage young people to collect things like stamps, postcards, leaves, dried flowers, or quotes they like. Contribute to their collections. • Ask young people to teach you a new skill or about a subject they're studying in school.
Ages 16 to 18	• Help teenagers think about their future goals and the discipline required to reach them. • Encourage teenagers to take an interesting community education class. • Place emphasis on lifelong learning and not just on graduation.

Pass It On!

Handout 15

Building the Positive-
Values Assets

All young people need positive values to help guide their choices. Here are ideas on how to build the six Positive-Values assets for children and youth at different ages:

Ages Birth to 1	• Create a caring atmosphere for babies at home, in child-care centers, and in other places. • Encourage families to talk about their values while modeling and teaching them as their children grow.
Ages 1 to 2	• Teach children to care for others, such as by sharing or giving hugs. • Interact with children in loving, respectful, and caring ways.
Ages 3 to 5	• Teach children how to care for special things, such as toys, outfits, or plants, by themselves. • Encourage parents to explain their values simply to children when they see others behaving in ways they value or do not value.
Ages 6 to 11	• Have children write thank-you notes or show their appreciation in some other way whenever they receive gifts. • Encourage families to participate in service activities together. • Talk to children about specific examples of people acting on their values.
Ages 12 to 15	• Interact in caring, responsible ways with people of all ages. Encourage youth to do the same. • Watch television or read books together and discuss the characters' values. • Talk to young people about your values regarding honesty; sexual activity; alcohol, tobacco, and other drug use; and other topics.
Ages 16 to 18	• Encourage teenagers to volunteer with at least one organization. • Together write letters to the editor of a local newspaper or to politicians about your views on issues. • Talk with teenagers about how their values guide their choices and behaviors. Let them know how your values influence you.

Building the Social-Competencies Assets

Young people—no matter what their age—need to develop social competencies. Here are ideas on how to build the five Social-Competencies assets for children and youth at different ages:

Ages Birth to 1	• Give babies new toys and safe objects to touch and explore. Infants learn a lot about how to deal with people by first interacting with objects. • Encourage children to experiment with sounds. It will help them develop language later on.
Ages 1 to 2	• Give children at least two equally appealing choices whenever possible. • Encourage children to express their feelings, but give them guidelines on appropriate and inappropriate ways to act on their feelings.
Ages 3 to 5	• Continue to cheer on children's new skills, such as drawing, walking backward, and learning how to cut with scissors. • Encourage families to start having periodic family meetings in which children have input in decision making. • Let children make simple choices on their own, such as whether to play with blocks or to color.
Ages 6 to 11	• Encourage children to use words—rather than just actions—to communicate. • Encourage children to develop more skills in areas that interest them. • Find ways for children to spend time with people who look, act, think, and talk in different ways.
Ages 12 to 15	• Help young people use healthy coping skills when difficult situations arise. • Be gentle and supportive in how you respond to young people's fluctuating emotions. • Help young teenagers find ways to deal with conflict without fighting.
Ages 16 to 18	• Slowly begin to allow teenagers more freedom to make their own decisions. • Ask teenagers about their dreams for the future and help them plan how to achieve them. • Encourage teenagers to practice healthy responses to situations where they might feel pressured or uncomfortable, such as being offered drugs by a friend or being challenged to fight.

Pass It On!
Handout 17

Building the
Positive-Identity Assets

All young people need to feel good about themselves and their abilities. Here are ideas on how to build the four Positive-Identity assets for children and youth at different ages:

Ages Birth to 1	• Always love, accept, and respect babies. • Play together with babies in ways that make them laugh and enjoy the time together.
Ages 1 to 2	• Create a loving, supportive, and affirming atmosphere for children. • Dwell on what children do right instead of what they do wrong. When they make mistakes or act out, focus on the behavior, not the child. For example, instead of saying, "No! You are so naughty," try saying, "No, it's not okay for you to do that."
Ages 3 to 5	• Break new tasks and skills into small, manageable steps that children can master without becoming too frustrated. • Talk with children about the good things that happen in their lives. • Find ways to teach children about their cultural heritage, such as through stories or special foods.
Ages 6 to 11	• When children are facing problems or difficult times, help them think of all the possible ways they could deal with the situation. Then help them pick what they want to do. • Encourage children to find inspirational, positive role models. • Talk with children about what gives your life meaning and a sense of purpose.
Ages 12 to 15	• Expect young people to experience ups and downs of self-esteem during these years. • Avoid comparing young people with each other.
Ages 16 to 18	• Let teenagers know that you are proud of and excited by their talents, capabilities, and discoveries. • Support teenagers as they struggle with issues and questions of identity. • Let teenagers know that you are willing to listen if they want to talk about their sense of purpose in life, including their ideas about how they would like to contribute to the world.

Pass It On!

Handout 18

Asset-Building Ideas
for Adults

All adults can help young people thrive by building their Developmental Assets. It doesn't necessarily take a lot of time or energy. Here are some easy ways to get started:

➤ Learn more about asset building. You can do this by attending a training session, reading about asset building, talking with others who know about the assets, and surrounding yourself with reminders about the importance of assets, such as the list of 40 Developmental Assets and photos of young people in your life.

➤ **Learn the names of children and teenagers who live near you or who work in shops or community centers you frequent. Greet them by name.**

➤ Model a positive, healthy lifestyle. This includes finding peaceful ways to resolve conflicts (asset 36); being motivated to achieve (asset 21); and advocating and working for equality and social justice (asset 27).

➤ **Support local efforts to provide safe spaces for young people to meet and spend time together.**

➤ Expect young people to behave responsibly. Let them know what you expect from them—before there is trouble. Compliment them when you see them doing good things.

➤ **Take time to play or talk with young people who live near you or work with you.**

➤ Commit to at least one act of asset building every day.

➤ **Support efforts to create or expand opportunities for children and youth to participate in teams, clubs, and organizations.**

➤ Build at least one informal, ongoing, caring relationship with a child or adolescent.

➤ **Examine your attitudes about children and youth. See young people as resources rather than as problems.**

➤ Thank people who work with children and youth (teachers, youth group leaders, social service providers, clergy, and others).

➤ **Organize a musical instrument drive to encourage people to donate used, but working, musical instruments to a school or youth program.**

➤ Look out for the children and youth around you. Help keep them safe. Report dangerous and inappropriate behaviors to parents, school officials, or law enforcement officers. Also, compliment parents when you see their children doing good things.

➤ **Get involved in volunteer efforts with children and youth. You can find these through local schools, youth-serving organizations, congregations, parks and recreation programs, and other community-based organizations.**

➤ Take time to nurture your own assets by spending time with supportive people, using your time constructively, and reflecting on your own values.

Asset-Building Ideas
for Senior Citizens

Growing older can bring many positive things: knowledge, wisdom, experience, perspective. Sharing some of this wealth with young people builds assets in a way that no other age group can. Whether you work outside the home or not, have grandchildren or don't, have a lot of money or a little, you can offer young people support, a sense of history, boundaries, and most important, a positive relationship with a caring adult. Here are some ideas for what seniors can do to build assets for children and youth:

➤ **Post the list of assets in your home.** Commit to doing something to build assets each day, week, or month.

➤ **Speak well of children to other adults.** If you hear people making negative generalizations about young people, don't let them get away with it.

➤ **Ask your friends about the children and youth in their lives.** If you have a chance to meet those young people, tell your friends what you like most about them.

➤ **Reach out to the children and youth in your family,** whether they are your grandchildren, great-grandchildren, nieces and nephews, grandnieces and grandnephews, or other relatives. Send letters, visit, call them, or invite them to your home. Let them know your door is open if they want or need you.

➤ **Start a "Round Robin" letter for your neighborhood or extended family.** Write a brief personal update, include a picture or two, and send it to one person. That person does the same thing and sends it to the next person, who adds their contributions. The letter keeps going around (getting thicker and thicker) until everyone has seen all of the entries. Encourage young children to enclose pictures they've drawn or a tape-recorded message.

➤ **Introduce yourself to the children and youth who live near you.** Learn their names and greet them when you see them.

➤ **Make spending time with children and youth part of your routine.** If you take a daily walk, greet young people you see along the way. When you're at the grocery store, smile at the young children and say hi to them.

➤ **Spend time with young people, doing things you enjoy.** If you like to crochet, teach a young neighbor how. If you like to tinker with cars, talk with the automotive teacher at a high school about volunteering in a class.

➤ **Volunteer at a child-care center, school, or faith-based youth program.** For example, one first-grade classroom had a man they called Grandpa Chuck who came to class on a weekly basis to listen to the children read aloud.

➤ **Become a foster grandparent** for a family that doesn't have grandparents or whose grandparents live far away.

➤ **Set boundaries for when you are willing to care for other people's children**—including your own grandchildren. You'll be a much better asset builder if you don't feel resentful or taken advantage of as a babysitter.

➤ **If your community has an asset-building initiative, get involved.**

➤ **If you had a special older person in your life when you were a child, think about the things that made that relationship special** and offer the young people in your life some of those same gifts.

Asset-Building **Ideas**
for Young People

You can make a difference for yourself and your peers by learning about and building the Developmental Assets. Some teenagers have started by learning the names of more of their peers at school. Some build assets by befriending younger children. Others have focused their efforts on making a difference in their congregation or community. Here are ideas on how to get started as an asset builder:

➤ Learn the names of your neighbors (including adults, children, and other teenagers). Ask one of your parents to introduce you to neighbors you don't know.

➤ **Post the 40 Developmental Assets in your room or in your locker. Choose a different asset each day and focus on nurturing it for your friends.**

➤ Sample a variety of experiences and activities in music, theater, art, and athletics, at school and in your community.

➤ **Participate in at least one club, group, team, or sport—or find something creative that appeals to you, like acting or music.**

➤ Get to know an adult you admire.

➤ **Replace put-downs with affirmations.**

➤ Write a note to or call one of the main asset builders in your life. Thank her or him for making a difference in your life.

➤ **Think of your best friends. Do they build you up or drag you down? How do they build assets for you? How do you build assets for them?**

➤ Go out of your way to greet your neighbors.

➤ **Limit the amount of television you watch. Choose shows you really like and not just whatever is on.**

➤ Volunteer at a local nursing home, community center, or animal hospital.

➤ **Take a conflict-mediation course.**

➤ Start a book club with friends and read just for fun.

➤ **Practice different ways of saying no when people try to get you to do things that you don't really want to do.**

➤ Talk about the 40 Developmental Assets with your family. Which assets do family members think are the strongest in your family?

➤ **If you have a part-time job during the school year, limit your work schedule to allow time for schoolwork, doing things with family and friends, and other activities.**

➤ Identify something each family member is good at and learn from them. If your sister is great at geography, turn to her when you're reading a map or needing help with a geography assignment. If your dad is a whiz at math, seek him out for making a savings plan or for assistance with a math problem.

➤ **Discuss with young people in your neighborhood what's good about where you live. Also discuss ways you could help improve the neighborhood.**

➤ Even if your family provides a warm, caring, supportive place to grow, also seek support through adults in your school, community organizations, or faith community. The more positive adult relationships you have, the better.

➤ **Examine the activities you are in outside of school. Are you feeling challenged? Do** you enjoy the activities? **Do you feel you have enough time to do the activities, complete your homework, and also have time for yourself, family, and friends? If not, consider making some changes.**

➤ Seek out adult mentors and healthy role models.

➤ **Become involved in a social issue that interests you, such as poverty, civil rights, endangered species, hunger, child abuse and neglect, the environment, or discrimination.**

➤ Get involved in the community through volunteering.

➤ **Build a relationship with a child through babysitting, playing catch with a neighbor, or volunteering as a coach or coaching assistant.**

➤ Let your friends know that you are available when they need someone to talk to. If they need it, help them get additional assistance from a counselor, social worker, parent, or other adult.

➤ **Seek out people and information to help make your future dreams and plans come true.**

➤ Remember that younger kids see you as a role model. Take time to say hi and talk to them when you see them, especially at school.

➤ **When you see someone being a bully, try to stop the bullying if you can do so peacefully. If necessary, take the problem to an adult.**

 **Pass It On!**
Handout 21

Asset-Building **Ideas**
for **Children**

Developmental Assets are the things all people need to be happy and successful in life. People of all ages can build assets. Here are ideas for how you can build assets:

➤ Say hi to people you know. Smile at them.

➤ **Help your friends when they need help.**

➤ Follow the rules that adults set. If you don't understand a rule, ask questions. If you think a rule isn't fair, tell someone.

➤ **Tell a friend about your day.**

➤ Play with a younger child. Play what that child wants to play.

➤ **Pick something to learn about. Look at books. Ask adults about the subject.**

➤ Thank people when they do something nice for you.

➤ **Tell people how you feel.**

➤ Teach somebody how to do something. Can you stand on your head? Whistle? Tie shoes? Do yo-yo stunts? Make up jokes?

➤ **Invite someone new to play with you and your friends.**

➤ Look at books with another child. Read aloud if you know how, or make up a story to go with the pictures.

➤ **Don't worry when you make mistakes. Everyone makes mistakes sometimes. Mistakes can help you learn.**

➤ Ask other people how they are feeling.

➤ **Volunteer to help someone do something.**

➤ Try a new, safe activity—even if you're not sure you'll like it.

➤ **When someone does something that hurts your feelings, tell that person. Explain why it made you feel sad.**

➤ If someone is being a bully to you or someone else, ask him or her to stop. If that doesn't work, tell an adult.

➤ **Give your family ideas of fun things to do together.**

Asset-Building **Ideas**
for Parents and Guardians

Being a parent or guardian can be very hard work—no surprise there, right? Most parents and guardians have things they love about their role as well as problems with their kids that they have to deal with. What might be surprising, though, is that one of the best ways to deal with problems is to focus on positives. Research shows that a more effective approach to raising healthy, competent kids is to concentrate on building Developmental Assets. These assets form the foundation young people need to make healthy choices and to succeed in life. The more assets your kids have, the stronger this foundation will be.

There are probably lots of asset-building things you already do for your children—even if you don't call them that. Here are some ways to be intentional about asset building:

➤ **Post the list of 40 Developmental Assets on your refrigerator door.** Each day, do at least one asset-building thing for each family member.

➤ **Connect with other parents who are interested in asset building.** Form relationships in your neighborhood, on the job, through a congregation, or through a parent-education organization.

➤ **Regularly do things with your child,** including projects around the house, recreational activities, and service projects. Take turns planning activities to do together as a family.

➤ **Eat at least one meal together** as a family every day.

➤ **Negotiate family rules and consequences** for breaking those rules.

➤ **Develop a family mission statement** that focuses on building assets. Then use it to help you make family decisions and set priorities.

➤ **Talk about your values and priorities,** and live in a way that is consistent with them.

➤ **Give your children lots of support and approval** while also challenging them to take responsibility and gain independence.

➤ **If you are parenting alone, look for other adult role models** of both genders who can be mentors for your children.

➤ **Nurture your own assets** by spending time with people who care about you and are supportive. Also, take opportunities to learn new things, contribute to your community, and have fun. You'll take better care of your children if you take care of yourself.

➤ **Think about the way you were parented** and how that affects your relationships with your children. If there are parts of your relationship with your parents that were very difficult or that get in the way of your parenting, consider talking with someone about these issues.

➤ **Keep all family members (including you) from watching too much television.** Find other interesting and meaningful activities for your children to do—some with you, some with their friends, some by themselves.

➤ **Learn as much as you can about what your kids need at their current ages.**

➤ **Recognize that children need more than just financial support.** They also need emotional and intellectual support. Balance family time with other priorities like work, recreation, and hobbies.

➤ **Don't wait for problems to arise before talking with your children's teachers.** Keep in regular contact with them about how your children are doing and what you can do to help your children learn.

➤ **Think of teenagers as adults in training.** Teach them something practical, such as how to change a tire on the car, prepare a meal, or create a monthly budget.

➤ **Be aware of differences in how you relate to your children.** Are you more comfortable with one gender? If so, why? What impact does that have in your family?

➤ **Talk to your children about the 40 Developmental Assets.** Ask them for suggestions of ways to strengthen their assets.

➤ **Do intergenerational activities** with extended family and with other neighborhood adults and families.

➤ **Be an asset builder** for other young people in your life.

➤ **Remember that you are not alone.** Other asset builders in your children's lives include coaches, child-care providers, faith-based education teachers, club leaders, and neighbors. Work with these people to give kids consistent messages about boundaries and values.

➤ **Get to know your children's friends, and the parents of their friends.** Talk to them about Developmental Assets.

Asset-Building **Ideas**
for **Grandparents**

Being a grandparent means different things to different people. Many children are being raised by their grandparents or spend a great deal of time with them. Other grandparents live in different states or countries than their grandchildren and rarely, if ever, see them. Whether you see your grandchildren daily or just once in a while, you can do many things to help nurture their assets. Here are some ideas for building assets for your grandchildren:

➤ **Support your children in their parenting.** There are different ways to do this, including telling them what you think they do well, giving them a break by babysitting once in a while, and being respectful of the way they do things (even if you'd do them differently).

➤ **Have clear boundaries and high expectations for how you expect your grandchildren to behave.** Also talk with your children about the boundaries and expectations they have for your grandchildren. Finally, talk with your grandchildren about how you hope they will behave and why those things are important to you.

➤ **Introduce your grandchildren to other caring elders,** such as your friends or other relatives. The more exposure older people and youth have to one another, the better able they will be to relate and get along.

➤ **Help make history come alive for your grandchildren.** Tell them stories about their parents and about your own life. Help them think about their future by talking about goals and dreams that you had as a young person.

➤ **Model lifelong learning by reading, taking classes or lessons, or trying new things.** Talk with your grandchildren about what you are learning and why it is important to you.

➤ **Model involvment in community service** (for example, planting a plot in a community garden or volunteering at an animal shelter). Talk about your experience and why you have decided to contribute to your community.

➤ **Attend school and community events** that your grandchildren are involved in.

➤ **If your grandchildren live far away, try to see them on a regular basis.** Also think of creative ways to stay connected with them at other times. Call them often, mail them notes, send e-mail messages, or tape record yourself reading them stories.

➤ **Spend some individual time with each grandchild.** Frequently tell them how special they are and how much you love them.

➤ **Avoid making comparisons among your grandchildren.** Enjoy what is unique about each one.

➤ **Play games with your grandchildren,** such as card games, board games, computer games, or made-up games.

➤ **Expose your grandchildren to cultural, religious, and family rituals.**

➤ **Give children enriching experiences with the arts.** For example, take them to concerts, theater productions, museums, or art exhibits.

➤ **Talk with your children about the boundaries they have for your grandchildren.** Work together to provide consistent boundaries—and messages.

➤ **Talk about your values, your priorities, and world issues that concern you.** Emphasize why these things are important to you and how they influence your life.

Asset-Building **Ideas**
for Brothers and Sisters

Having brothers and sisters can make life very interesting. Sometimes you probably fight or disagree. Other times you might be best friends. Brothers and sisters can also make life pretty good. Whether you love being together or drive each other crazy, you and your brothers and sisters can be important asset builders for each other. Here are some things to try:

➤ **Get to know your brothers and sisters better. Even though you may live together, you may not know each other well. Find out what you have in common and how you are different.**

➤ Don't tease your siblings. Even if it's just for fun, it might make them sad. Try to laugh *with* each other instead of *at* each other.

➤ **Talk about your roles in your family. Sometimes older children make decisions for younger children. Does that happen in your family? Why?**

➤ Think about each other's assets. Which assets are strong for you? Which need to be stronger? What are your brother's or sister's top 10 assets? What can you do to build assets for each other?

➤ **Commit to building assets in each other—and in your parents.**

➤ Know that all brothers and sisters sometimes have conflicts. Agree to solve conflicts peacefully. If you and your siblings need to learn how to do this, ask your parents or someone else to help you.

➤ **Thank your siblings when they do nice things for you.**

➤ The next time your brother or sister has a friend over, spend a few minutes with the two of them. Get to know your brothers' and sisters' friends.

➤ **If people compare you with your brothers or sisters, ask them to stop. Suggest that they point out your individual strengths instead.**

➤ Show your support for each other. For example, if one of your brothers or sisters plays a sport, go to a game once in a while.

➤ **Ask your brothers and sisters to teach you something. Maybe you have a younger sister who makes bracelets. Ask her to show you how to make one. Maybe your brother knows how to do cartwheels. Ask for some tips.**

➤ Do something nice for someone. You and your brothers and sisters could clean up your kitchen without being asked, or you could help a neighbor with a project.

➤ **Do something fun together, like tell jokes, read to each other, eat Popsicles, make a snow sculpture, play a board game, create a family play, build a tree house or fort, or go swimming.**

Asset-Building **Ideas**
for Neighbors and Neighborhood Groups

Aneighborhood is more than a place where people sleep or grab a bite to eat. A neighborhood can and should be an important community in which people of all ages feel cared for and secure. This kind of neighborhood isn't the norm in most communities, but with a focus on asset building it could be. Two of the 40 Developmental Assets (4: Caring Neighborhood; and 13: Neighborhood Boundaries) focus specifically on the important role neighbors have in building assets. Here are ideas on how neighbors can build these and other assets:

Individuals

➤ **Learn the names of kids who live around you.** Find out what interests them.

➤ **Treat neighbors of all ages with respect and courtesy;** expect them to treat you with respect and courtesy too.

➤ **If you live in an apartment or condominium, spend time in gathering places,** such as front steps, courtyards, meeting rooms, pools, laundry rooms, and lobbies. Greet and talk with others there. If you have a front yard, hang out there.

➤ **Take personal responsibility for building asset 13: Neighborhood Boundaries;** when you see someone in the neighborhood doing something you think is inappropriate, talk to her or him about why it bothers you. When you see someone doing something nice—picking up trash, for example—tell them how much you appreciate it.

➤ **Find other neighbors who want to make a long-term commitment to asset building.** Begin developing strategies for working together to build assets in your neighborhood.

➤ **Take time to play or just be with the young people** on your block or in your building. Encourage them to talk and then listen to what they have to say.

➤ **Invite neighbors (especially those with children and teenagers) to your home.** Get to know each other and find out what you have in common.

➤ **Once in a while, leave messages** (with chalk on sidewalks or by hanging notes on doors) saying how much you appreciate a certain neighbor. Do this for neighbors of all ages.

➤ **If you have children, talk to other parents about the boundaries and expectations they have for their children.** Discuss how you can support one another in areas where you agree.

➤ **Figure out what you can provide for young people in your neighborhood.** Can you set up a basketball hoop? Can you offer some space for a neighborhood garden? Can you give one hour of your time on weekends to play softball with young people who live near you?

➤ **If you have concerns about your neighborhood, talk with other neighbors about your feelings.** If others share your concerns, gather a group to work on addressing them. Even if you don't solve all of the problems, you'll strengthen your neighborhood through the process.

➤ **Attend a game, play, or event** that a neighborhood child or teenager is involved in. Congratulate the young person after the event.

➤ **Be aware of graduations and other major events** in the lives of children.

➤ **Once you know your neighbors, find out more about their extended family and friends.** Some elderly people have grandchildren who visit. Or parents may have custody of their children on certain days of the week. Get to know these young people who periodically visit.

➤ **Pay attention whenever you see a young person.** Take time to smile and say hello. If you have a few moments, ask a few questions and express your interest in her or him. Do this while you're walking, waiting for a bus, or waiting in line at the grocery store.

Groups

➤ **Start a neighborhood group.** Focus on safety, neighborhood improvement, or just having fun. Get young people involved in the group. They often have creative ideas and solutions.

➤ **Organize a neighborhood book swap.** Ask neighbors to donate books they've already read and have everyone come to find new books.

➤ **Meet with neighborhood parents and other concerned adults to find out how neighbors can help children and teenagers with homework.** Consider finding adult "study buddies" for kids.

➤ **Start a neighborhood check-in program.** Form small clusters and check in with each other on a regular basis. If someone needs help or support, gather a group to pitch in and help out.

➤ **If you have problems with crime or safety in your neighborhood, regularly talk with your local police department** to find out what is being done to address the issues. Ask them what you and other neighbors can do to make a difference.

Asset-Building **Ideas**
for Babysitters

Being a good (caring, responsible, fun) babysitter does more than build your financial assets. You build your Developmental Assets, including those in the Empowerment and Social Competencies categories. You also are an asset builder for the children in your care. Parents benefit too. They have someone they trust to be with their children while they work, take time for themselves, or do other important things.

So what does it take to be an asset-building babysitter? Here are some tips:

➤ **Learn as much as you can about the 40 assets and why they are important.** There are different lists of the 40 assets for different age groups.

➤ **Give children all of your attention.** Rather than turning on the television, popping in a DVD, or calling a friend, ask them to choose games to play or things to do.

➤ **Show parents that you are an asset builder.** Ask questions of parents and kids and show your interest in kids by smiling and saying hello to them when you arrive.

➤ **Have a backup adult whom you can call if you need help or support.** This could be your parent, neighbor, aunt or uncle, grandparent, or some other adult you know.

➤ **Ask the parents what boundaries they have for their children,** and how you can uphold these boundaries.

➤ **Check out age-appropriate books from the library before you babysit.** Ask a librarian for suggestions. Read these books to the children, or let them read to you.

➤ **Create a babysitting co-op** with a couple of reliable friends. A co-op is where you agree to sometimes refer parents to other babysitters you know, and they do the same for you.

➤ **Tell parents how much you charge before you take the job.** Then they won't be surprised or pay you less than you expected. If parents can't afford what you charge, you'll have to decide if you are willing to lower your rates.

➤ **Set good limits** for how many hours you will work and how late you will stay.

➤ **Learn about child development.** Playing should be the best part of babysitting. Understanding the ways children play at different ages will make your time together more fun.

➤ **Take first-aid courses** and make sure the parents give you emergency numbers so you can reach them.

➤ **Recognize how your role is different depending on the age of the children you're caring for.** Babies, toddlers, and preschoolers require intensive care and supervision. School-age children need supervision, but you can give them more opportunities to care for themselves.

➤ **Model nonviolence** and teach children to resolve conflicts without hurting others.

➤ **Wait until the kids have gone to bed to watch movies or shows that might be inappropriate for them.** If you're not sure what's OK for them to watch, ask their parents.

➤ **Have fun!**

Asset-Building **Ideas**
for Child-Care Providers

Each day brings new experiences in the life of a child as he or she learns new things. As children face the excitement and challenges of constant change, they look to the adults who care for them for guidance, nurture, stability, and structure. By focusing on building the 40 Developmental Assets, you help children grow in healthy, balanced ways, and you contribute to the foundation they need to be successful in life. Here's how you can be an asset builder for children:

➤ **Give each child one-on-one attention** at different times throughout each day.

➤ **Greet children and parents as they arrive,** even if you already have another child in your arms.

➤ **Learn about the 40 Developmental Assets and their implications** for the children you work with. Post the lists of assets for different ages and refer to them often.

➤ **Learn the names of family members of children in your care.** Make eye contact, smile, and call them by name when you see them.

➤ **Give children simple, age-appropriate activities** that encourage their independence and leadership. For example, have children take turns choosing a book to have read aloud during group reading times.

➤ **Limit exposure to TV.** If children watch TV, select only educational, age-appropriate programs.

➤ **Be consistent with the daily schedule.** Children feel more secure when activities occur at the same time each day.

➤ **Tell parents about asset building.** Give them the list of 40 Developmental Assets. Encourage them to post the list at home.

➤ **Point out positive, caring behaviors of**

children. When you see a child share a toy, express your approval.

➤ **Keep kids physically and emotionally safe.** Make sure they feel comfortable and valued.

➤ **Read to children every day.** Use puppets and other ways to make reading fun.

➤ **Because children learn by experience, give children opportunities to see, hear, taste, touch, and smell new things.**

➤ **Model calm and patience.** Children need to be taught how to deal appropriately with their emotions, and they also need to see adults acting in appropriate ways.

➤ **When children do things you don't like or you disapprove of, tell them why you don't want them to act that way** and what you would like them to do differently.

➤ **Encourage children to try new activities, but don't force them.** Some children warm up to new things slower than others.

➤ **Avoid comparing one child with another.** Every child is unique.

➤ **Celebrate the characteristics that each child brings to the group.** Find ways each child can shine.

➤ **Remember to take good care of yourself because caring for children is hard work.**

Asset-Building **Ideas**
for Teachers

To teach is to touch a life forever. Teachers have the potential to be powerful asset builders. In addition to the Commitment-to-Learning assets (21–25), five other assets (3: Other Adult Relationships; 5: Caring School Climate; 8: Youth as Resources; 12: School Boundaries; and 14: Adult Role Models) focus on the important role of a teacher. Below are some suggestions for what teachers can do to build assets. These suggestions are intended to give you some ideas for how to get started. They may need to be modified or adapted depending on the grade you teach; whether you are a classroom teacher, specialist, or resource teacher; and the nature of your school environment.

Asset Building in General

➤ **Post the list of assets** in your classroom.

➤ **Devote a bulletin board in your classroom to asset-building messages.**

➤ **If your community has an asset-building initiative, get involved.**

➤ **Train all volunteers and support staff you work with to use the asset framework.**

➤ **Plan asset-building learning activities as part of the curriculum** (for example, service learning projects, social skills training, or setting aside time to read for pleasure).

➤ **Put an asset-building message on your computer screen saver.** One school used the slogan, "Wrap Your Arms around Cherry Creek Kids . . . Build Assets!"

➤ **Greet students by name** when you see

Support

them.

➤ **Send a letter to parents about the idea of asset building,** and then use assets as springboards for discussions in conferences with parents and students.

➤ **Meet with other teachers and brainstorm ways to help students succeed.** A school in Wisconsin set up DATES (Developing Assets to Encourage Success) meetings that are designed to help students who are struggling academically.

➤ **Encourage access to at least one caring adult for each student** in the building. Homerooms can facilitate this.

➤ **Provide asset-building resources for parents.**

Empowerment

➤ **Teach students about the 40 assets and help them set goals for assets they want to develop** (two resources for this are *Me@ My Best* and *Take It to the Next Level*, published by Search Institute).

➤ **Provide opportunities for service-learning.** Help students plan and make decisions about providing service to others.

➤ **Empower students by encouraging them to tell their stories** through written and visual autobiographies.

Boundaries and Expectations

➤ **Work with students to set school boundaries or rules.** Post a written set of the rules in conspicuous places: hallways, classrooms, the lunchroom, the gymnasium, and other common areas. Create copies of the rules and have an agreement form for students and parents to sign, indicating their willingness to stay within the boundaries.

➤ **Set high and clear expectations** for student behavior and learning outcomes.

Constructive Use of Time

➤ **Create visual symbols of assets.** For example, cooperative murals can show the importance of working together to strengthen the community. Art students can create self-portraits that reflect their assets.

➤ **Thank other teachers, staff, and students when you catch them building assets.**

➤ **Demonstrate sensitivity with respect to student involvement in extracurricular activities.** Some teachers make it a practice to always allow at least two nights for students to complete assignments.

➤ **Read biographies or view films about musicians and other artists.** Discuss the assets students see in these people's lives.

➤ **Discuss current music, movies, or arts and entertainment and the messages they send.** Do they build assets or not?

Commitment to Learning

➤ **Discuss the assets of characters in stories, history lessons, and current events.** For example, when studying *Romeo and Juliet,* talk about how asset deficits can lead to tragedies. Change the tale by building assets for the two main characters.

➤ **Use assets as the focus for assignments.**

➤ **Choose a quote of the day with an asset focus** and ask students to talk about it.

➤ **Introduce students to Web sites that have asset-building themes.**

➤ **Read biographies of people who have realized their dreams.** Talk about the assets that helped those people succeed.

Positive Values

➤ **Ask students to gather information about their heroes—famous or not.** Then have small-group or class discussions about what values these heroes seem to have and how those values guide who they are and what they do.

➤ **As a class, create a list of shared values.** See the Positive-Values assets (26–31) as a place to start. Talk about what it takes to uphold these values. Set boundaries and expectations based on these values.

Social Competencies

➤ **Provide a process in the classroom for mutual goal setting and evaluation.** Such a process empowers students and actively engages their learning.

➤ **Encourage planning through the use of student agendas and calendars.**

➤ **Use resources in your community to help teach Cultural Competence** (asset 34). Consider having students organize a diversity-awareness week, a cultural fair, or some other way of learning about each other's backgrounds and cultures.

➤ **Don't let students get away with bullying or fighting.** Talk to them about how to resolve conflicts peacefully.

Positive Identity

➤ **Use "strength interviews" with students to help them identify their assets** and their sources of support.

➤ **Attend concerts, programs, and activities** your students are involved in.

➤ **Congratulate successes** with a written note, a call home, or verbal praise.

➤ **Create life-planning portfolios** that follow a student from the end of one school year to the beginning of the next school year and include goals, dreams, and hopes. They can be an important tool for the student—and for teachers—to keep track of accomplishments and challenges.

Asset-Building **Ideas**
for School Administrators

The challenge of asset building in schools is to give each student not only a support person but an entire support system. While school structures and systems vary, administrators can use their influence and position to transform schools into environments that are rich with asset-building occurrences and relationships. In addition to the five Commitment-to-Learning assets (21–25), four assets (5: Caring School Climate; 12: School Boundaries; 14: Adult Role Models; and 16: High Expectations) show the connection between an educational system and the health and well-being of young people. Here are some ideas on how school administrators can build all of the assets:

Asset Building in General

➤ **Provide professional development for staff members** in asset building.

➤ **Dedicate a few minutes at each staff meeting to share asset-building stories, information, strategies, and ideas.**

➤ **Encourage your school board to proclaim an asset-building week** within the community.

➤ **Include asset building in your school's mission and goals.**

➤ **Add an assets column to the school newspaper.** Include students as writers, editors, and reviewers.

➤ **If your community has an asset-building initiative, get involved.**

➤ **Create a fax cover sheet that has an asset-building message on it** (for example, "You have the power to make a difference for children").

➤ **Leave a message about asset building on your voice mail** (for example, "…please leave your name, number, and a brief message, and remember, you can make a difference in a child's life today").

➤ **Train teachers and other staff in asset building** and use the assets as part of performance planning and evaluation.

➤ **Print and distribute stickers and buttons that say "I am an asset builder!"**

➤ **Print asset-building tips on check pay stubs.**

➤ **Support and underwrite the cost of the *Search Institute Profiles of Student Life: Attitudes & Behaviors* survey** in your district so that the community has an accurate assessment of young people's assets, deficits, risk behaviors, and positive behaviors.

➤ **Distribute information about the assets to all teachers.** Consider purchasing asset-building resources for each employee or for a resource library.

➤ **Take advantage of grant opportunities that could support asset-building initiatives in the district.** Engage parents with skills in grant writing to help with the process.

➤ **If your school or community has an asset-building initiative, paint the logo on buses,** create a banner to hang on school buildings, or run messages about the initiative on the school marquee.

Pass It On!
Handout 29

Support

➤ **Create mentoring programs for staff as well as students.** It can increase school bonding and provide needed support.

➤ **Share information about Developmental Assets with parents.** Resources for this include the *Ideas for Parents* newsletters and *Bring It On Home: Connecting Parents, Kids, and Teachers* from Search Institute.

➤ **Create an environment that welcomes students, staff, and visitors.** Have student and staff greeters at the doors. Keep the building clean. Invite parents and other community members to visit. If safety is an issue, work with your local law enforcement to keep the building as secure as possible

Empowerment

without giving it the feel of a prison.

➤ **Recruit community groups and individuals to volunteer** time to build assets in your school(s).

➤ **Thank staff and students** whenever you see them building assets.

➤ **Include students on interview teams for personnel selection.** Students can provide tours to informally assess candidates and/or take part in the official interview.

➤ **Include students** on school-improvement management teams, disciplinary teams, and other working groups.

Boundaries and Expectations

➤ **Clearly state rules for appropriate behavior and consequences for violating those rules.** Post them in visible places.

Constructive Use of Time

➤ **Make extracurricular activities like theater, sports, clubs, and academic teams a priority.**

➤ **Celebrate successes.** Whether it's a commendation in the announcements, a personal letter to a student, or a pat on the back, catch staff and students doing things well.

Commitment to Learning

➤ **Encourage scholarship contributors to establish criteria and select recipients based on students' asset-building efforts as well as other achievements.**

Positive Values

➤ **Work with parents, teachers, board members, and others to create a list of shared values for the school.** See the Positive-Values assets (26–31) as a place to start. Integrate these values into lesson planning, external communication, and boundaries and expectations for behavior.

Social Competencies

➤ **Provide agendas and calendars for students** to help them with planning and decision making.

Positive Identity

➤ **Support and attend recognition banquets** and other ways of honoring students.

Asset-Building **Ideas**
for Student Support Staff

A s a school counselor, social worker, librarian, nurse, or other student support staff member, you come in contact with many students every day. While you won't be able to develop a relationship with each of them, there are things that are unique about your role that make you a key asset builder in your school. You can link students with other resources in the school or the community, you can be an adult in the school whom young people can talk to when they need extra support or advice, and you can provide students with information that can help them take care of themselves well and plan for the future. Even if you only see most students once in a while, there are steps you can take to build assets. Here are some ideas:

➤ **Post the list of assets** in your office or work area.

➤ **Greet students** whenever you see them—in or out of school.

➤ **Use the asset language** when talking with students, parents, or other staff.

➤ **Use the asset model** as part of any assessment and goal setting you do with youth.

➤ **Whenever you talk with parents, be sure to tell them what you like about their kids.**

➤ **When dealing with students who are struggling, work as many sincere compliments into the conversation as possible** (even if it's just one).

➤ **If your community has an asset-building initiative, get involved.**

➤ **Build your own assets;** you'll be better able to deal with your students if you take care of yourself.

➤ **Thank students** when you see them building assets for their peers.

➤ **Help coordinate information nights and orientations** to help students and parents locate classrooms, meet staff, learn about the services you provide, and ask questions before school begins in the fall.

➤ **Start a peer-helping program.** For example, offer new student support groups to help stu-

dents adjust to a new environment. Those who graduate from the group can lead the group the next year.

➤ **Offer student-assistance programs that reflect an asset-building focus.** For example, when working with recovering chemically dependent students, focus as much on future plans and goals as you do on staying sober.

➤ **Involve students in strength interviews as they process challenges in their lives.** Ask questions such as: Who can you count on? What keeps you going? What inner resources do you have to draw on? Who can you turn to when you need extra support?

➤ **Serve as a liaison with the local radio and television stations** to share with your community the good news about your school.

➤ **When discussing specific students with other staff, focus as much on their personal strengths as on challenges.** If you believe in students, others will start to believe in them as well.

➤ **Work with teachers to incorporate asset assessment and development into group and classroom guidance activities.** For example, a career unit could include an interview where students talk about which assets they think they most need for on-the-job success.

Asset-Building Ideas
for School Support Staff

Support staff—adminstrative assistants, paraprofessionals, teaching assistants, and others—are key to the climate in a school. They have daily interactions with students and they can sometimes focus on building relationships with young people in ways that teachers and administrators cannot. Thus, school support staff have lots of asset-building potential. Here are ideas on how support staff can build assets:

➤ **Post the list of assets** in your work area or office.

➤ **Learn about the assets and talk about them** with others. Speak well of students, and speak warmly to them.

➤ **Do at least one thing each day to intentionally build assets.**

➤ **Ask your supervisor if you can attend professional development opportunities** related to asset building.

➤ **View interruptions by students as your most important work.** It may not always be efficient, but taking the time to talk with and help students will make your school a better place.

➤ **See yourself and your colleagues as part of a web of support for young people.** Be flexible with time and duties so that students feel comfortable approaching you for help, advice, or other kinds of support.

➤ **View your activities within the asset framework.** If you are supervising the study skills laboratory, for example, help students develop the Commitment-to-Learning assets (21–25).

➤ **When supervising the hallways or lunch area, focus on positive values.** If students cut in line, remind them of the importance of being a role model (15), being honest (29), and having integrity (28) as you uphold school boundaries (12).

➤ **Show genuine enthusiasm for a job that allows you to work closely with and for young people.** If you don't like your job, talk to your supervisor or a trusted colleague about what you can do to make it better.

➤ **Laugh a lot.** While anyone can complain, it takes a creative person to rescue difficult situations with humor.

➤ **Notice what's working.** Tell a student directly when he or she did something right. Send a note to a teacher when he or she did something you admired.

➤ **Greet students** by name.

➤ **Attend student activities** and tournaments.

➤ **Get involved with other organizations that build assets** in children and youth.

➤ **Send notes to young people commending their efforts** as well as their successes.

➤ **Call parents with news of positive and helpful behavior** you see in their children.

➤ **Compliment young people on even the smallest positive behavior,** such as picking up another student's book when it fell or smiling at someone.

➤ **When participating in or observing a student activity (such as track or band), take pictures.** Get double prints and give the students the second copy.

Asset-Building **Ideas**
for **School Bus Drivers**

Transporting children and youth from place to place is a big responsibility in terms of Safety (asset 10) and the Boundaries-and-Expectations assets (11–16). You also can make the experience a positive time for yourself and your passengers by focusing on asset building. Here are ideas on how to get started:

➤ **In addition to paying attention to safely transporting students, think of yourself as an adult role model** for them.

➤ **Post the list of assets** on your bus.

➤ **Be clear from the first time students ride your bus about the behavior you expect from them.** Know what consequences you can enforce and who you can go to for support.

➤ **Get to know the names of the young people who ride on your bus.** Greet them when they get on and off the bus.

➤ **If you regularly drive for the same team or group of young people, get to know them.** For example, if you drive the swim team whenever it has a meet, drop in on a meet and watch the young people swim. Talk with them afterward about how it went.

➤ **Hang up newspaper clippings and pictures of young people who ride your bus in the front of the bus.** One bus driver plastered the area above his windshield with photographs, mementos, and news clippings about students. The riders loved seeing their pictures. Some even drew pictures for the bus driver to hang up in the bus.

➤ **Make the atmosphere on the bus supportive and fun within safety limits.** Talk with the kids, play music that is appropriate for young people, tell them jokes.

➤ **Get to know the bullies on the bus.** Take a course in peaceful conflict resolution (asset 36), and—based on what you learn—talk with the bullies about alternative ways to act around other young people. Let them know you won't tolerate bullying.

➤ **Talk with other drivers about creative solutions to problems** and how to make buses places to build assets.

Asset-Building **Ideas**
for Educators in Faith-Based Organizations

Chances are good that one reason you agreed to teach a faith-based education class is that you care a lot about young people and want to see them thrive. Your commitment to young people and your involvement in their lives can have a big impact on their Developmental Assets as well as on their spiritual growth. Here are some things you can do to help build their assets:

➤ **Show each young person in your class or group that you care about her or him.** Greet each one personally. Notice when they are absent. Say hi to them outside of the education hours.

➤ **Create a climate in which young people's opinions and experiences are valued and respected.**

➤ **Let children and youth help choose and adapt the curriculum** you use.

➤ **Connect classroom learning with service to others.** Have your class play with or read books to children in the nursery. Have your class prepare and teach a class to younger children about peaceful conflict resolution.

➤ **Be clear about how you expect the young people in your class or group to behave.** Set and enforce clear and fair ground rules. Teach young people the boundaries and behaviors that are integral to the life of a believer in your faith tradition.

➤ **Create meaningful activities for young people that help them stretch and grow,** not just fill up the time you have together. You can start by involving them in planning and leadership.

➤ **Make lessons interesting, engaging, and relevant to young people's lives.** Be creative not only with the content but also with the format. Do some hands-on activities or games that teach and are fun. Take the young people on a short field trip during your time together.

➤ **Give young people opportunities to learn, practice, and teach social competencies.** Role play different ways to respond to situations. Tie in a passage from a sacred text to a specific Social-Competencies asset, such as asset 33 (Interpersonal Competence), which is about friendship and treating others well.

➤ **Help shape young people's personal identity** by helping them internalize their faith and discover their own sense of purpose.

➤ **Find other teachers who are interested in asset building.** Meet regularly to share ideas, discuss problems and possibilities, and celebrate what's working in your classroom.

➤ **Nurture your own development as a teacher and a person of faith.** Build on the strength of the assets you have.

Asset-Building **Ideas** for
Youth Workers in Faith-Based Organizations

Major goals of youth workers in faith-based organizations are to address young people's spiritual needs and to ground them in the faith tradition. Asset building can be an important part of nurturing a faithful, value-centered person. A caring, welcoming environment that supports young people and challenges them to grow will keep young people involved and interested in your faith. Here are some suggestions:

➤ **Learn about the asset framework.** Make a commitment to building assets for youth in your faith community—and for all the children and young people around you.

➤ **Plan a youth program that intentionally addresses one or more of the assets.** For example, plan a series of events focused on the Positive-Values assets (26–31).

➤ **Nurture your own assets.** Surround yourself with people who support you and your work. Empower yourself by serving others. Set boundaries on your time and high expectations for yourself. When you spend time with young people, do it because you really want to, not because you feel you have to or should. Uphold positive values. Build your own social competencies. Focus on what excites you about youth work and dream big about the future.

➤ **Identify how your programs and activities already build assets.** List all the formal and informal opportunities your faith community offers for young people and evaluate each in light of the asset framework.

➤ **Nurture an asset-building climate in your youth group**. Focus on creating an atmosphere that is warm (where young people, volunteers, and youth leaders are friendly and welcoming), caring, thinking (where young people are challenged to think and grow), and valuing (where young people are valued and respected).

➤ **Train all volunteers and other youth workers in the asset framework.** Discuss the unique implications that asset building has for your faith community.

➤ **Ensure that retreats, camps, and trips are asset-building experiences by balancing fun with learning and by building relationships.** Expose young people to new people, cultures, experiences, and opportunities to learn about themselves and their abilities. Take time after these experiences to reflect on what happened—the positives and the negatives—to help young people process what they learned.

➤ **Form partnerships with other people who are interested in building assets.** Some of these people may be members of your faith community; some may be part of a different faith tradition; others may be in a youth-service organization or school. The important thing is to find other caring adults who want to bring out the best in young people. By working together, you'll develop creative ideas, be able to expand your outreach, and make a bigger difference in the lives of kids.

➤ **Involve youth in asset-building efforts.** Include them on planning teams, ask for and use their ideas about programs and activities, and build relationships with them by working together to build assets for all young people in your faith community.

Asset-Building **Ideas**
for **Volunteer Coordinators**

As a person who works with volunteers, you know that there is a lot more to volunteer coordination than just scheduling. Volunteers need training, encouragement, and feedback on the work they are doing. Volunteers who work with youth can be great asset builders, and you can help them by providing the support they need. Here are some things you can do:

➤ **Recognize that some potential volunteers are uncomfortable around children and youth.** Provide training in different skills such as listening, leadership, and conflict resolution. Ask volunteers what other skills they would like to strengthen or develop to help them feel more confident about working with youth.

➤ **Give each volunteer a list of the 40 assets that focuses on the age-group he or she works with.**

➤ **Create volunteer notebooks filled with practical information about youth.** Notebooks could include sample lessons, typical behavior of young people and how to respond, articles that address specific topics related to your work, quieting-down activities, and class rosters. Some places create one or two office notebooks, others provide them for each activity or each volunteer.

➤ **Be creative with volunteer training.** Send one or two volunteers to a workshop and have them come back and train other volunteers (this is a way to empower and give leadership skills to volunteers). Assign a related book for volunteers to read and then have a book discussion. Or one person could read a book and write a review of it for others.

➤ **Establish clear boundaries for volunteers** working with children and youth.

➤ **Screen volunteers who will work with children and youth.** Know the potential risks of this kind of volunteering and do what you can to minimize them.

➤ **Talk with people in the community to learn about barriers to volunteering with children.** You could conduct written surveys, hold focus groups, or do phone surveys. Based on what you hear, take steps to do things that encourage people to get involved and make the barriers seem smaller.

➤ **Talk with volunteer coordinators in other programs about how they can and do incorporate asset building** into their program.

➤ **Post your volunteer opportunities through VolunteerMatch on the Web (www.volunteermatch.org),** an organization that lets nonprofit groups, schools, congregations, and other organizations post their information free of charge. Then publicize your involvement in that Web site.

➤ **Create a job description for each volunteer position you have.** Be specific about details, including title of volunteer position, basic objectives and responsibilities, skills and experience needed, time commitment, training required, and to whom the volunteer reports.

➤ **Create youth-oriented volunteer opportunities that are diverse in the amount of time, energy, and expertise needed.** Someone who has never volunteered before may be more comfortable making a short, one-time commitment than a time-intensive, ongoing one.

➤ **Affirm volunteers.** Go out of your way to visit with them and tell them you appreciate their contributions. Provide opportunities for the young people to thank them. When their volunteer commitment is over, honor them in some way.

➤ **Spend time with volunteers,** provide supervision and feedback, provide opportunities for growth, and give them opportunities to get to know one another.

➤ **Build a diverse team of volunteers.** Recruit females and males of different ages, races, and socio-economic backgrounds.

➤ **Show volunteers the connections between the 40 Developmental Assets and the purpose of your program.** For example, in tae kwon do, not only are you providing a youth program but you're also building self-esteem, personal power, and caring relationships and you are teaching resistance and peaceful conflict-resolution skills.

➤ **Assess if your organization can involve children and youth as volunteers.** Service is an important component of asset building, and young people need high-quality volunteer opportunities.

Asset-Building Ideas
for Mentors

Mentoring relationships can be found in all different walks of life among people of many different ages. Working adults sometimes have a more experienced coworker or supervisor who serves as an adviser or teacher. Young children often have an older sibling, tutor, or friend who acts as a trusted guide and confidant. Many teenagers learn from and are supported by a youth worker, teacher, religious leader, or coach. All of these relationships can be called "mentoring" and all of them have the potential to build assets. While asset building is likely to happen naturally when a mentoring relationship develops, there are some things you can do to ensure that your mentoring relationship is an asset-building one:

➤ **Remember that the focus of mentoring is on forming a relationship** and being a positive adult role model. *What* you do matters less than the fact that you are spending time together and providing the person you mentor (your "mentee") with support and care.

➤ **If you are part of a formal mentoring program, understand and honor the boundaries set by the program.** Some, for example, expect the mentor not to discuss the mentee at length with family members. Others ask for at least a one-year commitment. If you are uncomfortable with the guidelines set by a particular program, talk with the leaders about why the boundaries are the way they are.

➤ **Have clear boundaries for what is appropriate and not appropriate in your relationship.** For example, it may be acceptable for your and your mentee to go on a one-day outing alone together but not to go somewhere overnight. If you are not sure what's OK and what's not, talk first with the leaders of your mentoring program. You might also talk to your mentee's family, friends who also mentor, a religious leader, or another trusted person.

➤ **Show your mentee that he or she is a priority by keeping in touch or getting together on a regular basis** (such as monthly, biweekly, weekly, or daily). Even if you cannot be together very often, write letters, talk on the phone, or send e-mail.

➤ **Let your mentee know that you care about things that are important to her or him.** For example, if your mentee has a special friend or pet, ask regularly about how he or she is doing. If your mentee plays a sport, attend a game or match. If he or she sings or plays an instrument, ask for a personal recital or go to a concert.

➤ **Be flexible.** If your mentee has ideas about things to do or ways to do them, let her or him take the lead. You don't need a careful plan to build assets.

➤ **Meet and get to know your mentee's family.** Once you know them, they will likely have more trust in you, and you will have a better understanding of your mentee's life experiences.

➤ **Get to know your mentee's interests and hobbies.** Help her or him find opportunities to get involved with organized activities or programs that use or develop those interests and hobbies. For example, if he or she likes writing poetry, look for creative writing classes or workshops through community education or youth programs.

➤ **Talk about and model your personal values.** Encourage your mentee to think about the values that are important to her or him and how those values impact behavior and decisions.

➤ **Share a new experience together, such as fishing, visiting a local museum** (some have days where entrance fees are waived or reduced), taking a class, eating at a new restaurant, watching a movie and talking about the asset-building themes in it, flying a kite, renting a canoe or paddleboat, snow-shoeing, or hiking.

➤ **Practice life skills together.** For example, prepare a meal and eat it together.

➤ **Emphasize the importance of a lifelong commitment to learning.** Go to the library together and check out books to read together. Also look for books on tape that you can listen to together. Help your mentee with homework or find someone who can.

➤ **Bring the arts into your mentee's life.** Go to an art museum, play, or symphony concert.

➤ **Talk about some of your hopes and plans for the future and ask about your mentee's vision of the future.** Share ideas with each other about how you can make your respective dreams come true. If it seems like your mentee's dreams can't or won't come true, work together to come up with ways to deal with barriers.

➤ **Enjoy your time together and have fun!**

Asset-Building **Ideas**
for Coaches

Coaches teach young people not only the rules and strategy of games but important lessons about life as well. You can help young people develop confidence and self-esteem, help them learn to resolve conflicts peacefully, teach them ways to take care of their health and well-being, and help them develop skills for communicating with others. Here are a few ways coaches can be asset builders:

➤ **Learn the names of all the players on your team** and call them by name. Make a point to talk at least once with each player each time you practice or play.

➤ **Create and maintain a positive atmosphere.** Two top reasons young people participate in sports are to have fun and to spend time with their friends. It's not all about winning.

➤ **Focus on helping players get better, not be the best.** It will reduce players' fear of failure and give them permission to try new things and stretch their skills.

➤ **Know that highly competitive sports can often cause a great deal of stress for young people.** The intense pressure that goes along with trying to be the best can sometimes lead to unhealthy outcomes such as substance abuse and/or eating disorders. Be careful not to push young people too hard and learn about the warning signs of possible problems.

➤ **Care about your athletes' lives outside of the sport** and show them that they are valuable people as well as team members.

➤ **Adapt your teaching style and language to the players' age level.** Young children do not always know sport terms. Use words and concepts they understand. On the other hand, older youth may be more successful when they understand the big picture of what they are trying to accomplish as well as the specific skills or strategies needed.

➤ **Set goals both for individuals and for the team.** Include young people in setting these goals.

➤ **Catch kids doing things right.** Be quick to praise a player's efforts. The best feedback is immediate and positive.

➤ **Use the sandwich method of correcting a player's mistake.** First praise, then constructively criticize, then praise again.

➤ **Always preserve players' dignity.** Sarcasm does not work well with young people. They may not always remember what you say, but they always remember how you said it.

➤ **Insist that all team members treat one another with respect.** Then model, monitor, and encourage respect. Have a zero-tolerance policy for teasing that hurts someone's feelings.

➤ **Be specific about a code of conduct and expectations** for athletes, parents, spectators, and team personnel.

➤ **Encourage athletes to do well in school** and to be motivated to achieve.

➤ **Respect other activities and priorities in athletes' lives.** Avoid conflicts with their other commitments and respect their need for time with their families.

➤ **Find ways each child can participate,** even if he or she is not particularly skilled in the sport.

➤ **Listen to and encourage your athletes' dreams, concerns, and desires—**sports-related or otherwise.

➤ **Develop leadership skills in young athletes** by giving them opportunities to lead practice drills and develop a team code of conduct.

➤ **Take time at the end of practice to have the group offer positive comments about each player's performance that day.** Make sure no one is left out.

➤ **Split up cliques on the team** by mixing up groups for drills or scrimmages.

➤ **Plan a community service project for the team.** It teaches players to give something back to the community.

➤ **If you have an end-of-season gathering, take time to say a few positive things about each player.** Avoid Most Valuable Player awards and other "rankings." Focus on the relationships, the improvement of the team, and the unique contributions of each player.

Asset-Building Ideas
for Police Officers

Police officers play a unique role in our society because they're entrusted with considerable power to uphold the law while also creating a presence of safety. Becoming an asset-building police officer can add a new dimension to the job, a dimension that often is overlooked. Here are ideas on how to start building assets:

➤ **Learn as much as you can about the 40 Developmental Assets.** Use the list in thinking of ways to deal with juvenile offenders and also criminals who have children.

➤ **Keep the assets in mind when making arrests.** Recognize that many offenders have few assets and have not had many experiences interacting with asset builders.

➤ **Learn as much as you can about the community you work in.** Identify areas of strength and safety besides areas of crime. Consider doing asset analysis in addition to doing crime analysis.

➤ **When handling family disputes or arguments between people, encourage peaceful conflict resolution.** In addition to intervening when conflicts come to a head, think of ways to help people build the skills to deal with their anger and prevent violence.

➤ **Build relationships with people in the community.** Become a visible presence in the neighborhoods where you work. Attend events such as neighborhood block parties or school plays to get to know the people.

➤ **Give "positive tickets" to young people when you see them doing good things.** In Jackson, New Jersey, police officers issued 200 tickets for free ice cream cones to children who wore protective helmets while riding bicycles. "It makes for a positive first contact with police," says the sergeant in charge.

➤ **Target high-crime areas to build assets.** Have a police officer set up an office in the area to build strong relationships first with young people and then with the parents, neighbors, and finally the schools and community. Find others within the area to partner with to build assets.

➤ **Consider ways to build assets off the job.** One Baltimore, Maryland, officer becomes J.J. the Clown during off hours and visits children in the hospital. He also uses his amateur puppeteer and magician skills to connect with young people.

➤ **Volunteer to visit a school to talk about safety.** Emphasize how safe the community is instead of how dangerous it is. Talk about the type of calls you get the most. Young people often think that police officers are constantly having high-speed chases and arresting murderers. Let them know about the other roles you play in the community.

➤ **Work with families with teenagers to create "safe houses" (houses that will host teenage parties where liquor won't be available).** Bring parents together to discuss ways to stop alcohol from being served at teen parties and how to create parties that teenagers will enjoy.

➤ **With other officers, eat lunch with the students at a local school on a monthly basis.** Get to know them and talk with them about what it's like to be a police officer.

Asset-Building **Ideas**
for Health-Care Providers

While most of your interactions with patients are probably brief and episodic, you can make the most of those times by building assets for your young patients and for the children of your adult patients. You'll probably enjoy it, and adults and young people alike will leave your office feeling good about themselves, about you, and about your organization. You'll also be helping young people thrive and be well; the more assets they have, the more likely they are to lead healthy lifestyles and avoid risky behaviors. Here are some ideas for what health-care providers can do to build assets:

➤ **Pay attention whenever you see a child or teenager—whether they're in your care or not.** Take time to say hello. If you have a few moments, ask questions and express your interest in the person.

➤ **Turn your waiting room into an asset-building area.** Have toys and books for younger children, magazines for older children, and notebooks for teens and adults that include information about asset building. If your community has an asset-building initiative, include information about it in the notebook.

➤ **Collaborate with schools and youth-serving organizations** to provide health care/healthy lifestyle information to young people.

➤ **Support local asset-building efforts** with financial, human, or in-kind resources.

➤ **Learn the names of your patients.** Ask them what they prefer to be called, note that in their charts, and then use those names throughout your visits.

➤ **Learn the names of your employees' and coworkers' children.** Regularly ask about how their children are doing.

➤ **Look patients in the eyes when you talk with them.** If an adult patient has a child accompanying her or him, get down on the child's level and engage the child in a short conversation.

➤ **Share information about asset building with parents,** especially new parents.

➤ **Keep track of some personal information about each patient.** For example, if you learn that a young person loves soccer, make a note of it. When the patient returns, scan these notes and ask about how the soccer playing is going. Keeping track of personal details not only gives a better picture of someone's health, but it also helps you make a quick personal connection.

➤ **Be respectful of patients' time and other commitments.** If you're running behind, ask your staff to inform patients of the delay as soon as they arrive.

➤ **Build relationships with chronically ill patients or patients who need care often.** Learn their names and a little about them so you can engage in conversation without having to consult a chart.

➤ **Empower patients by telling them how you are going to examine them before you actually do so.** Ask them how they're feeling if you detect any hesitation on their part. For example, don't assume a patient is experienced or comfortable with giving blood.

➤ **If your organization has a community advisory group or board, include young people.**

➤ **If your organization has a mission statement, add a statement about a commitment to young people.**

➤ **Host an "asset-building day"** and invite young people (children of employees, students, participants in a neighborhood youth program) to visit your organization for a day.

➤ **Offer young people opportunities to learn** more about working in a health-care organization through volunteering.

➤ **Host a community event focused on health and health care.** One community hospital has annual "health challenges." They give young people a tour, teach them some health-care basics, and let them help out with several tasks. The same community also holds a "health bee," where young people are asked questions about health care. Once kids are finished, they go across the street to a recreational facility where they can swim, play sports, and eat snacks provided by nutritionists.

➤ **Audit your human resources policies to be youth- and family-friendly** (such as flexible scheduling, time off to volunteer or take care of family, tax-deferred day-care payment options).

➤ **Consider how you can be an asset builder not only in the office but also after hours.** In what ways do you enjoy connecting with children and youth? What interactions and activities fit best with your schedule? What unique skills or interests can you share with a young person?

Asset-Building **Ideas**
for Media **Professionals**

Television, radio, movies, newspapers, the Internet, and other media have a major role in shaping people's attitudes toward and perceptions of young people. For some adults, it is their only exposure to children and teenagers. For children and teenagers, it gives messages about how adults perceive them and how they are "supposed" to act. Thus, those who work in the media have great potential and responsibility for sharing the message about the power of Developmental Assets. Here are a few tips on how media professionals can promote asset building:

➤ **Post the list of Developmental Assets** at your desk or in your work space.

➤ **Recognize your role in creating a community climate in which children and youth are valued, cared for, and supported.**

➤ **Balance negative stories about youth with positive coverage of young people** and their contributions. For example, when developing local angles for national stories about teenagers (which often focus on problems), find ways to highlight local solutions that focus on strengths.

➤ **Pay attention to the sometimes hidden stories of people giving their time, energy, and creativity** to improve the lives of children and youth.

➤ **When covering stories that involve youth, interview young people.** You may get interesting information and opinions, and you build assets in the process.

➤ **Give young people their own voice** through newspaper sections, television shows, or radio programs run by young people.

➤ **Cover the 4-H competitions** at county or state fairs.

➤ **Develop a "youth poll."** Survey young people on community issues such as curfew, adult attitudes toward youth, or alcohol and other drug use. Base a story or series on the results.

➤ **Focus a public service campaign on assets** or ways the community is meeting the needs of children and youth.

➤ **In analyzing trends, policies, and legislation, emphasize their potential long-term impact on young people.**

➤ **Pair up with the local library during the summer** to sponsor and highlight a summer reading program.

➤ **Develop an internship or mentoring program for students interested in media careers.** Or volunteer at a high school to teach students skills that you use on the job.

➤ **Make sure your colleagues understand the asset-building model and act on it.** Place asset-building material and posters in common areas. Be an advocate for positive attitudes about young people, both personally and professionally.

➤ **Sponsor a youth sports team.** Host a season-end party for players and their families.

➤ **Provide a strong editorial voice on behalf of issues that relate to children, families, and asset building.**

Asset-Building Ideas
for Store Owners/Managers

Small gestures can go a long way toward making children, youth, and families feel like important customers in your store. You can play an essential role in asset building by being a good role model, letting young people know that they are valued members of the community, and developing caring relationships with regular young customers. Here are a few tips on how to build assets:

➤ **Post the list of 40 Developmental Assets** in your store.

➤ **Treat all customers with respect.** Children and youth sometimes say that merchants avoid them and don't take them seriously as customers. But kids can be very savvy about where they spend their money. If they think you don't like them, they probably won't frequent your store.

➤ **Learn the names of repeat customers of all ages.**

➤ **Wear a name tag with your first name on it** and introduce yourself or make conversation when working with customers.

➤ **If you have a parking lot for your store, designate some front spots for pregnant mothers and for people with small children.**

➤ **Place information about the Developmental Assets into bags** with receipts.

➤ **If you advertise, consider using part of your advertising space to celebrate children, youth, and asset building.** One grocery store started picturing an asset-builder-of-the-week in its weekly newspaper advertisement.

➤ **Teach your employees about the assets** and encourage them to try to treat customers in an asset-building manner.

➤ **Support your community's asset-building initiative by getting involved or donating something from your store** that would be of use for the initiative or as prizes for a community event.

➤ **Set boundaries for store behavior** and merchandise returns. Have these boundaries posted and available for customers.

➤ **If you have teenage employees, treat them as you do your adult employees.** Have clear guidelines and expectations for professional behavior and provide adequate training. Give them support and encouragement to do their best. Also, celebrate their successes outside of work, such as good grades or winning a game.

➤ **Find ways to promote the asset-building projects of young people.** On the advice of an 8-year-old, one store sold quilt squares to be decorated for a community-wide quilt that was sewn together during a family-activity day.

➤ **Print asset-building messages on your store's bags.**

➤ **If you have a marquee, put asset-building messages on it.**

➤ **Donate unsold items to a local shelter, free store, or other organization that serves children.**

Asset-Building Ideas
for Real Estate Agents

People who know about and study assets are often heard to say, "Everyone can build assets." While it's true that individuals have personal capacity for asset building, there are many ways that people can build assets in their professional lives as well. For a real estate agent, this can mean connecting people to neighborhoods and communities in asset-building ways, taking time to get to know the children of your clients and learn about what they want from a home, and taking action to improve and strengthen the communities in which you work. Here are some asset-building ideas for real estate agents:

➤ **Learn as much as you can about the communities in which you help people buy and sell homes.** Gather information about the schools, neighborhood groups, businesses, and community organizations, and create packets to give to potential buyers.

➤ **Find out if the communities in which you work have asset-building initiatives.** If so, gather information about these initiatives, including the list of 40 assets, to give to potential buyers.

➤ **Model honesty, integrity, caring, and responsibility** in your work.

➤ **If a potential buyer has children or youth, talk directly with the young people** about what their hopes are for a new home.

➤ **Find out names of neighborhood coordinators (or block captains) for the communities in which you work.** When someone buys property, give her or him the name, address, and phone number of a neighborhood coordinator. Contact the coordinator to let her or him know about the new neighbor and the moving date.

➤ **When selling property, don't emphasize only the home and property values but** also the value of the community, schools, community organizations, community services, and other unique aspects of the area.

➤ **Really get to know the people you work with.** Find out about their hopes for neighborhood connections, their interest in young people, and what they enjoy doing. The more people you get to know over time, the easier you will find it to link individuals with organizations and other people in the community who have similar interests.

➤ **Encourage communities to develop community resource directories** that list organizations, annual community events, and services the community provides for families and individuals.

➤ **Get involved in asset-building projects to strengthen neighborhoods.** Strong neighborhoods are attractive to potential buyers and may help sellers move their homes more quickly.

➤ **Get involved in an asset-building initiative.** Talk about the trends you see in buying and selling homes in the community and the implications your work can have for asset building and vice versa.

Asset-Building Ideas for Organizations
Handouts 43-54

Asset-Building **Ideas**
for Any Organization

No matter what the specific mission of your organization is, you can build assets and make a difference in the lives of children and youth. Whether your organization has direct contact with young people or not, your interest in and commitment to an asset-building vision are what is important. Here are some ideas about how your organization can build assets:

◆ **Post the list of assets in key, high-traffic areas** throughout your buildings or sites.

◆ **If your community has an asset-building initiative, make an organizational commitment to support it** through financial, human, or in-kind resources. If your community doesn't have an asset-building initiative, take a leadership role in getting one started.

◆ **Shape your programs and services to advance the asset-building vision.** Even if your programs and services have little direct impact on children and youth, think of the indirect ways you touch young people. Use an asset-building perspective to examine and improve your policies, programs, and services.

◆ **Make your internal practices asset building.** Create a positive, supportive climate throughout your organization. Encourage employees' or members' involvement in asset-building programs and services. Create family-friendly policies that promote asset building and productivity.

◆ **Educate staff people or members about asset building.** Brainstorm and strategize about the implications that asset building has for your organization.

◆ **Network with other organizations within your community on behalf of young people.** Identify what expertise and resources each one could provide to make the community an asset-building one for all children and youth.

◆ **Be creative.** Asset building is about unleashing the creative ideas of individuals and organizations. What new perspective, approach, or idea could make asset building come to life in your organization—and in your community?

◆ **Be an advocate.** Many organizations play pivotal roles in shaping policies (both public and corporate), advocating for appropriate changes and increased asset-building opportunities within the community. Think about how your organization's leadership, staff, and constituency can advocate for asset building.

◆ **Provide support.** Asset building thrives when there's an undergirding of support, which includes the investment of time, money, and energy. How can your organization provide essential support to maintain asset building long term?

◆ **Recognize and celebrate asset-building actions.** If your organization publishes an in-house newsletter, write articles about asset builders within your organization. If not, send article ideas and photographs of asset builders to the community newspaper.

Asset-Building **Ideas**
for **Schools**

Schools have a unique opportunity to promote asset building. Often, they are at the center of community life, providing families with shared experiences that connect them to one another. In communities with highly transient populations, schools are frequently the *only* formal institution or service connected with families. Thus, schools have tremendous potential and responsibility for doing more than just transmitting information to students. When schools fulfill their leadership potential and use their unique position to be advocates for children and families, facilitators of partnerships and collaborations, and creators of safe spaces, they become asset builders for the entire community. Here are some ways to create an asset-building school or school system:

Asset Building in General

◆ **Support administration of the *Search Institute Profiles of Student Life: Attitudes and Behaviors* survey in your district.** Share results with the community and enlist its support.

◆ **Use the Developmental Assets as a tool** for performance planning and evaluation.

◆ **Create asset-building task forces in each building** to inform staff, students, and families about the asset-building model and to develop strategies to actively promote asset building. Include students, teachers, administrators, unlicensed staff, and volunteers.

◆ **Encourage your school board to pass a resolution supporting asset building** and to make a commitment to promote it within the school system and the community.

◆ **Include information on asset building in each school newsletter.** Remind readers that everyone can build assets; it is about every individual doing what he or she can to make a difference for young people.

◆ **Educate parents about the assets** and use the asset language when talking with them about their children.

◆ **Share the asset-building model with coaches and other extracurricular leaders.** Make asset building part of the philosophy guiding extracurricular programs.

◆ **Use assignments, class discussions, and projects to promote asset building.**

Support

◆ **Keep class sizes small** to give teachers and staff more time with each student.

◆ **Encourage teamwork.**

◆ **Offer parents easy and convenient ways to get involved** in their children's education (asset 6). For example, one-time activities such as tutoring high school students right before exam time can be perfect for a parent who wants to volunteer but cannot commit to regular involvement. For parents who never come to conferences, have an educator call them or go to their homes to meet with them.

◆ **Create a parent-education program** that starts by serving breakfast to families. When the students start their class day, invite the parents to stay for a message on parenting or child/adolescent development. Also offer learning opportunities during evenings or following conferences. Consider offering bus rides to parents who do not have transportation.

◆ **Invite senior citizens to have lunch with students.** It's a wonderful way to civilize a cafeteria and it helps students to connect with adults in the community.

◆ **Work with your parent/teacher organizations to build an educational component into their activities.** Encourage them to bring in speakers on parenting and child/adolescent development.

◆ **Assign each class a building-maintenance or cleaning project that requires them to work with the custodians.** It will sensitize the students to the care of the building and build bridges between the custodial staff and the students.

Empowerment

◆ **Engage students as leaders and decision makers,** including getting their input on school board decisions.

◆ **Seek learning opportunities that take students out into the community** and bring community resources into the classroom as well.

◆ **Invite students to discuss their school experiences with the school board.**

Boundaries and Expectations

◆ **Expect everyone to do her or his best.**

◆ **Set high standards for how students and staff are expected to behave.** Be consistent about following through with consequences when these standards are not met.

Constructive Use of Time

◆ **Work with congregations and cultural groups in your community to avoid scheduling school events that conflict with families' religious or cultural commitments.** Find out if your community has a calendar of events to help with this planning. If not, consider creating one.

◆ **Avoid scheduling practices or meetings that conflict with the dinner hour.** It is important for families to eat together.

◆ **Provide constructive before- and after-school programs for young people who would otherwise spend the time unsupervised** (and probably lonely). One way to do this is to link with existing programs and help expand them through financial, human, or in-kind resources.

Commitment to Learning

◆ **Have administrators greet students and staff at the door** each morning. The connection will create a caring environment (asset 5) and reinforce the commitment students and staff have to one another (asset 24).

◆ **Create a visual reminder of asset building.** For example, one school made an assets quilt that they hung in a prominent central location.

Positive Values

◆ **Work with parents, teachers, board members, and others to create a list of shared values for the school.** See the Positive-Values assets (26–31) as a place to start. Integrate these values into lesson planning, external communication, and boundaries and expectations for behavior.

Social Competencies

◆ **Train all students and staff in nonviolent conflict resolution.**

◆ **Open your building to community groups and organizations** during non-school hours.

Positive Identity

◆ **Focus on students' long-term goals as well as short-term assignments and projects.** Help students develop plans and visions for the future and the skills to make those dreams come true.

Asset-Building **Ideas**
for Faith-Based Organizations

All communities of faith are in a unique position to not only nurture and support the faith and spiritual development of young people but also to build Developmental Assets. Faith communities have the potential for intergenerational relationships; they provide opportunities for youth to grow and understand themselves; they reach and work with parents; and they have a public presence with the potential for leadership, advocacy, and service. Here are some asset-building tips for faith-based organizations:

◆ **Post the list of assets in key, high-traffic areas** throughout your building.

◆ **If your community has an asset-building initiative, get involved.** If there isn't an initiative, take a leadership role in getting one started.

◆ **Integrate asset building into your gatherings in ways that fit with the specifics of your faith tradition.** Create experiences for entire families. Think about how to include children and youth.

◆ **Provide a variety of educational opportunities for all ages.** Create interactive, intergenerational sessions that encourage younger people to connect with older people.

◆ **Provide opportunities for young people to volunteer in the community.** Afterward, discuss the experience from your faith perspective.

◆ **Reinforce positive values and morals.** Talk with young people about why these are an important part of your faith tradition.

◆ **Plan ways for families and other intergenerational groups to spend time together,** such as having a weekly or monthly meal, picnics, dances, concerts, or sports tournaments.

◆ **Collaborate with other faith-based and youth-based organizations** to learn about and build assets.

◆ **Provide responsible, meaningful roles for youth.** These could include being teaching assistants for young children, volunteering for child care, and pledging financial support from their allowances and part-time jobs, as well as worship activities, such as handing out bulletins, serving as readers, and being involved in music or other aspects of your faith tradition's gatherings.

◆ **Make your facility an asset-building place.** Rent or provide free space for children and youth clubs to use when your building is typically empty. Create a homework room for children and youth to hang out in after school, particularly if many are going home to empty houses. Host a neighborhood child-care center.

◆ **Educate your staff and lay leaders—in addition to the members at large—about asset building.** Discuss the implications that asset building has for your faith community, and brainstorm ideas together.

◆ **Create a book study group** that gives children, youth, and adults opportunities to read and reflect on books with asset-building teams.

Asset-Building **Ideas** for
Child-Care Centers

Millions of children spend time each day or week in some sort of child-care center. Parents, and indeed our entire society, rely on these centers to provide children with safe, appropriate environments. Thus, child-care centers have a major influence over our youngest generation. By focusing on the 40 Developmental Assets that all kids need, these centers can go beyond simply providing care. They can become stimulating, nurturing places that provide the foundation young people need for success in life. Here are ideas on how to build assets in child-care centers:

◆ **Learn as much as you can about the 40 Developmental Assets for the age of children your center serves.** Post lists in all the rooms in your center, and train staff in the Developmental Assets.

◆ **Make asset building part of your core curriculum** and policies.

◆ **Schedule annual or semi-annual conferences with parents.** Although it can be time consuming to prepare for conferences, they can help build relationships with parents while educating them about how their children are growing and developing. They also give you a chance to learn more about the children in your care.

◆ **Assign each child a particular child-care worker** so that each child has at least one adult with whom to form a close relationship.

◆ **Have written job descriptions that include asset-building language** for each paid and volunteer position. This helps people know what's expected of them.

◆ **Hang children's artwork and projects not only in rooms but also in the hallways and entrance to your center.** Consider framing some of them.

◆ **Take time to plan your programming,** and make planning a priority. Have weekly themes for activities, and give staff a regular, paid time to plan and prepare.

◆ **Share decision making among staff and volunteers** so that everyone feels supported and empowered to make decisions while also keeping each other informed.

◆ **Deal with difficulties and conflicts immediately,** before they escalate into large problems.

◆ **Make cultural diversity a priority.** Provide multicultural books, dolls, and toys for children to play with. Invite people from different cultures to visit and lead culturally specific activities with the children. Build a diverse staff.

◆ **Give child-care workers training and education throughout the year** so they can keep adding to their knowledge, skills, and creativity.

◆ **Publish a family newsletter on a monthly basis,** with the help of a volunteer, parent, or staff person who enjoys doing newsletters. Besides providing news about the center, include the names of all the child-care workers, their scheduled times, and the names of the children in each room. This helps parents to learn the names of people in your center.

◆ **Honor staff members, volunteers, and parents** for the contributions they make.

◆ **Set high expectations for your center.** Aim for national accreditation through the National Association for the Education of

Young Children (1509 Sixteenth Street NW, Washington, D.C. 20036; 800-424-2460; www.naeyc.org) or the National Association for Family Child Care (5202 Pinemont Drive, Salt Lake City, Utah, 84123; 800-359-3817; www.nafcc.org).

◆ **Create a bulletin board that includes a photograph and brief description about each staff person,** including your cook, custodian, and volunteers. This helps people put names with faces and encourages people to build community.

◆ **Advocate for high-quality child care,** not only for your center but for child care in general.

◆ **Develop asset-building days or asset-building weeks for your center.** Have asset-building activities during the day and send home a list of ideas on how parents can build assets for their children.

◆ **Employ and empower teenagers** by offering them the chance to care for younger children.

Asset-Building Ideas
for Libraries

Libraries and those who work in them can do more than nurture asset 25: Reading for Pleasure. In fact, libraries have tremendous potential to make a difference in the lives of young people. By giving young people access to books, computers, classes, and caring adults, libraries can open up a world of asset-building possibilities. Here are some ideas for what libraries can do to build assets:

◆ **Use the asset framework as a guide** when setting organizational priorities and goals.

◆ **Create displays that promote asset building** in general or your community's specific asset-building initiative. Post the list of assets in high-traffic areas of the library.

◆ **If your community has an asset-building initiative, offer the library as meeting space** for leadership teams, special committees, or other groups.

◆ **Train librarians, support staff, and volunteers to understand their role as asset builders.**

◆ **Design bookmarks with asset-building messages** to distribute to patrons.

◆ **Display artwork, inventions, and other projects of children and youth in your library.** Publicize the display in your community newspaper.

◆ **Develop planning and decision-making roles for young people,** such as including them on the library's board or creating a teen advisory group.

◆ **Create library internships for youth.**

◆ **Distribute lists of books with asset-building themes.**

◆ **Hold community workshops on how to choose asset-building books,** videos, and other materials.

◆ **Offer workshops for parents on how important it is for children to read and be read to.** Offer suggestions of specific books that might be appropriate for different age groups.

◆ **Create book groups where people can come together to discuss books.** Offer groups for children, teenagers, adults, and intergenerational groups.

◆ **Invite local authors to speak** about their writing and the role they think asset building has in the subjects they write about.

◆ **Create a community book chain** where each patron writes her or his favorite books on a piece of paper, and then link the pieces together to form a long chain in your library.

◆ **Encourage reading by having a community-wide read-a-thon.** Figure out ways to recognize participants in asset-building ways.

◆ **Work with educators who are book lovers** to develop asset-building reading programs and services.

◆ **Find storytellers in your community** and invite them to read, tell stories, or create dramatic presentations for children and youth.

◆ **Sponsor an event,** such as a poetry reading, planned by and offered to teenagers.

Asset-Building **Ideas** for
Organizations that Employ Young People

Bring out the best in the young people who work with you by doing things to build assets. Building assets in the youth you employ not only gives them essential skills but also makes them well-rounded, competent people. You benefit by having healthy, competent workers. Here are some ways to build assets in your employees:

◆ **Encourage the development of basic skills, such as writing, reading, mathematics, science, technology, and communication.** Show how these skills are important in your organization.

◆ **Take a personal interest in your young employees.** Share with them your personal interests and hobbies. Ask about theirs.

◆ **Teach young people skills you need them to perform** by modeling and explaining those skills.

◆ **Tell young people what you expect them to do and how you expect them to act when they are working.** When they act inappropriately or make mistakes, correct them gently while showing them appropriate alternatives for the future.

◆ **Give young employees a lot of feedback.** When you are not satisfied with their work, let them know how they can improve. Be sincere in your praise when young people have worked hard to earn it.

◆ **Point out the positive values that your organization believes in.** Explain why these values are important to you and the organization.

◆ **Provide adequate support for employees.** This includes orientation, training, supervision, criticism, and praise. For many young people, the job with your organization is their first work experience. Many do not know what to expect. Give them the big picture about what your organization does as well as the details of their jobs.

◆ **Use the "sandwich" model when you have a problem with an employee:** First praise, then talk about the problem, then praise again.

◆ **Offer young people opportunities** for advancing within the company.

◆ **Be clear about how young people can spend their time when work is slow.** One fast-food restaurant gives employees time to do homework during their work shift.

◆ **Invite young people to conferences, workshops, or seminars.** Explain why these continuing education opportunities are valuable.

◆ **Most young people have a strong desire to please the adults around them.** Don't exploit this. Teach young people how to take personal pride in their work.

◆ **Refer to the list of 40 Developmental Assets often.** Think of creative ways to build these assets for and with young people.

◆ **Acknowledge major accomplishments and milestones in young employees' lives,** such as graduation, or academic or sports achievements.

◆ **Create schedules that allow young people adequate time to do their schoolwork and participate in other activities.** Studies show that young people are most successful when they work 15 or fewer hours per week during the school year.

Asset-Building **Ideas**
for Businesses

Whether for profit or nonprofit, businesses have a lot of influence when it comes to asset building. Enriching the lives of children and youth not only is good for society in general, but it also can be good for business. Asset building strengthens the community, which is good for business, and asset-rich young people become productive employees and customers. Here are some ways businesses can build assets:

◆ **Post the list of Developmental Assets in high-traffic areas** throughout your organization.

◆ **Make it possible for all employees (parents and nonparents) to engage in asset-building efforts** by offering flexible scheduling, tax-deferred child-care payment options, time off for volunteering, and other family- and youth-friendly policies and benefits.

◆ **Build partnerships within the community to build assets.** Consider linking up with a school, a child-care center, a youth organization, or a preschool to give employees some focused ways to connect with children and youth. For example, employees could play and read for 30 minutes once a month with a group of 4-year-olds at a preschool, or they could tutor students in a subject related to their jobs for an hour every other week at a nearby high school.

◆ **Offer internships for youth** with concrete learning opportunities, good supervision, and plenty of support and guidance.

◆ **Use the asset framework as a resource** for employee training and development programs.

◆ **As part of your company's efforts to build goodwill and corporate responsibility, assume a leadership role in community-wide asset-building efforts.** If a community-wide initiative doesn't exist, become partners in and advocates for such an initiative, so that the community can become a healthy place for children and youth.

◆ **Support local youth development programs** through financial donations, human resources, and in-kind contributions.

◆ **Train employees in the Social-Competencies assets** as well as in the competencies and skills that your business requires.

◆ **Participate in mentoring programs** that pair adults and young people.

◆ **Be intentional about nurturing the 40 Developmental Assets** in the lives of teenagers employed by your company.

◆ **Focus corporate giving on programs that promote Developmental Assets** in the community.

◆ **Include asset-building tips in your company newsletter** and in paycheck envelopes.

Asset-Building **Ideas**
for Juvenile Justice Organizations

Juvenile justice workers know too well what happens when young people lack the developmental foundation they need. "Asset building works for kids in the system," said one advocate for an approach to juvenile justice that focuses on rebuilding that foundation in the kids who need it most. He believes that people who work with juvenile offenders need to ask themselves one key question: "How do we rebuild assets in these kids who didn't get them along the way so they can come back and be productive members of society?" Here are some ways to get started:

◆ **Focus on strengths.** In building case plans, assess the young people's and families' strengths as well as their needs. Everyone has some assets, but juvenile justice systems tend to focus on deficits instead. It is empowering to both youth and families to point out strengths and to identify concrete things that can be done to build on those strengths.

◆ **Relationships are key.** Programs and services by themselves don't change behaviors. Research shows that kids need strong bonds with caring adults. As a reminder of this, post the list of Developmental Assets on your office door and do at least one asset-building thing for each youth or family you work with each day.

◆ **Be a team player.** No one person, program, or service is the answer. Parents, teachers, employers, mentors, religious youth workers, and others can and should help support the youth and families you deal with. Be a leader in bringing this support system together.

◆ **Share the asset message with colleagues** in law enforcement, probation, courts, and youth services. Demonstrate how assets provide concrete actions to counter "risk factors."

◆ **Explore how the asset framework may be used to support innovative approaches to juvenile justice** such as the balanced and restorative justice approach, community con-

ferencing, victim-offender mediation, restitution, community service, mentoring, and other innovative approaches.

◆ **Encourage courts and juvenile services to provide free drop-in child care** for the children of offenders who are in court or receiving services.

◆ **Train community members in how to interact and build positive relationships in asset-building ways with youth offenders** as well as other young people they deal with.

◆ **Working with others in the community, help offenders discover opportunities to experience success,** build their skills and competencies, and increase their confidence.

◆ **Work with others to identify, reduce, or eliminate factors in your community that put youth at risk for delinquency,** school dropout, teen pregnancy, substance abuse, and violence.

◆ **Be an advocate for a healthy community**—a definable group, region, or network that organizes its systems and invests its resources to consistently promote Developmental Assets in all its young people. As a juvenile justice professional you can credibly make the "pay now or pay more later" argument.

Pass It On!
Handout 51

Asset-Building **Ideas** for
Service Clubs and Fraternal Organizations

With a commitment to community service and often a focus on children and youth, service clubs and fraternal organizations have a lot to offer in the way of asset building. They can use their leadership and their access to many different sectors to greatly influence the attitudes and actions of people within the community. Here are some asset-building ideas:

◆ **Invite speakers to talk about asset-building topics on a regular basis.** Consider opening some of these events to the public.

◆ **Use your access to many sectors in the community to promote, inform, and support asset-building efforts.** Work to create new asset-building ventures that are creative and make a difference for children and youth in your community. For example, in Hudson, Wisconsin, the Rotary Clubs spearheaded the creation of a youth-designed, youth-governed park to give kids recreational activities in an asset-building environment. The result was a 22,500-square-foot outdoor park.

◆ **Invite leaders** in schools, youth-serving organizations, and children's organizations to be part of your organization.

◆ **Sponsor intergenerational community events,** such as community-wide picnics and ice cream socials. Or have a community kite-fly; you could give away kites to kids and have kite-flying demonstrations, displays, and classes.

◆ **Encourage members to find ways to build assets** through their own professional affiliations and in their personal lives.

◆ **Support asset-building initiatives** and programs through benevolence funding.

◆ **Create an asset-building library** for the community.

◆ **Invite youth speakers to come and talk** about what it's like to be a young person in your community.

◆ **If you have an international focus and international connections, use them** as an opportunity to build cross-cultural connections and relationships and to explore multiculturalism.

◆ **Encourage members to be mentors or to do volunteer activities** through schools or youth-serving organizations.

◆ **Consider supporting an asset-building venture in your community** through service, leadership, or financial resources. In some communities, service clubs and fraternal organizations have been the main initiators and supporters of local asset-building efforts.

◆ **Recognize and publicize outstanding asset builders in the community.** Consider giving a monthly or annual award.

Asset-Building **Ideas** for
Corporate and Philanthropic Foundations

How foundations shape their guidelines for funding often determines to a significant extent how communities pursue the public good. In this way, foundations shape public consciousness about what matters. Here are some things foundations can do to help ensure that asset building becomes a top priority:

◆ **Revise grant-making guidelines to include a focus on positive outcomes.** Several foundations have revised their grant-making guidelines to establish development of the 40 assets as the primary criterion for giving.

◆ **Encourage and equip employees to build assets** in their own networks and spheres of influence.

◆ **Work with asset-building grantees to establish reasonable methods of evaluation** that are consistent with the asset-building approach.

◆ **Include youth in grant-making roles within or through the foundation.** One foundation provided a grant to a group of young people who in turn gave mini-grants to students who wrote proposals for asset-building activities. The Student Service and Philanthropy Project, a partnership between the New York City Schools and the Surdna Foundation, trained and supported youth in establishing student-run foundations. For information, go to: www.learningtogive.org/materials /sspp.

◆ **Examine how the foundation's practices model asset building in the community.** For example, does the process for grant seeking empower applicants, or does it make them become overly dependent upon outside funding?

◆ **Train board and staff members in the Developmental Assets** and the implications they have for your foundation and its work.

◆ **Provide impetus and leadership for asset building.** Link up with other leaders within the community, and work together to promote, educate, and lead asset-building efforts.

◆ **Focus on the human resources of your foundation in addition to the financial resources you provide.** How can the people within the foundation build assets and promote asset-building efforts?

Asset-Building Ideas
for Community Newspapers

Local newspapers play a unique role in the community. They can help build a sense of connection by reporting on local events and people. They also serve as a community voice and often provide the leadership that helps communities find shared values, commitments, and hopes for the area. Thus, these local publications can be strong vehicles for advocating policies, programs, and ways of life that promote asset building in the community. Here are some ideas for getting started:

◆ **Invite a parenting educator from the school system** to write a weekly column on parenting.

◆ **Start a monthly tabloid section that revolves around asset-building efforts.** Work with youth workers, educators, and others to generate written material and art that addresses asset-building issues.

◆ **Create a high school preview special section that highlights the school athletic teams, bands, debate teams, and other groups each season.** Advertisers tend to support these sections, and they provide an opportunity to get hundreds of young faces in the newspaper.

◆ **Highlight a "student of the week" or other young person to honor.** Include information about the young person's life outside the activity being highlighted. Make arrangements for a local restaurant that caters to youth to display the article.

◆ **Create a community calendar that has an asset-building theme.** Work with the local chamber of commerce and schools to collect all of the important dates for your community. Sell advertising to support its development. Publish it at a time that makes sense for your community, such as just before the school year begins.

◆ **Incorporate asset-building messages** into your front page on a permanent basis.

◆ **Create small filler ads that promote specific assets or the general asset-**building concept** to use when you need to square off the layout of paid advertising.

◆ **Create house ads that remind the community what asset building is** and why it is important.

◆ **Start a youth page and hire youth to work on it.** Cover youth achievements and events on a regular basis and give young people space to express their ideas and opinions about issues that are important to them. This kind of recognition and input helps youth feel valued and part of the community. It also gives adult readers and reporters an opportunity to hear from and about young people.

◆ **Make a long-term commitment to spreading the asset message.**

◆ **Give young people recognition for doing positive work in the classroom.** Print your schools' honor rolls or find other ways to acknowledge high achievers.

◆ **Find a high school student to write an opinion column periodically for your regular opinion page.** Help adults learn what the community looks like through the eyes of a youth.

◆ **If you have young newspaper carriers, highlight one each month with a photo and short profile in a house ad.** Write the young person a letter praising her or him for the effort. Top off the recognition with free tickets to the local movie theater.

◆ **Invite your local foundation or organization to sponsor a weekly youth asset-building column.** It would be great exposure for the sponsoring organization and a good way to keep the asset-building message in front of the public each week.

◆ **Offer to send your editor and advertising director to work with the middle school English or social studies class to create a newspaper.** It's a great way to introduce young people to the print media, and the youth-generated product gives the students another means of expressing themselves.

◆ **Offer tours of the newspaper office and the printing plant** to youth groups and classes.

◆ **Put a new asset-building message on the front of your newsstands each month.**

◆ **Print bookmarks with asset-building information** on them and provide them to the public library and local bookstores for distribution.

Asset-Building **Checklist**
for Your **Organization**

There are a number of ways your organization can build assets. You can build assets internally through policies, practices, and procedures, and externally through involvement in the community and support for asset-building initiatives and efforts. While this is not a scientific assessment, you can use this checklist to see how you're currently building Developmental Assets as well as to identify areas you could strengthen.

Vision, Mission, and Values	We already do this	We could do this better	We're unable to do this
1. Does our mission statement reflect a focus on or commitment to children and youth?	☐	☐	☐
2. Do our mission and goals reflect a commitment to the overall well-being of the community in addition to our specific initiative?	☐	☐	☐
3. Do we consider the impact on children and youth as we make major decisions and do strategic planning?	☐	☐	☐
4. In trying to make our vision a reality, do we focus primarily on long-term outcomes, not just short-term results?	☐	☐	☐

Asset-Promoting Programs			
5. Do our programs reflect the principles of asset building?	☐	☐	☐
6. Have we identified all the ways our programs may impact or engage *all* young people, regardless of gender, ability, race, ethnicity, culture, sexual orientation, and socioeconomic status?	☐	☐	☐
7. Do children and youth feel welcomed in our organization?	☐	☐	☐
8. Do we make intentional efforts to build intergenerational relationships?	☐	☐	☐
9. Do we provide opportunities for children and youth to develop assets through service projects?	☐	☐	☐

Evaluating Employee Policies			
10. Do we have flexible policies that help parents balance family and parenting responsibilities with the work, such as flexible scheduling, parental leaves, and on-site child care?	☐	☐	☐

	We already do this	We could do this better	We're unable to do this
11. Do we encourage our employees to volunteer in schools, recreational activities, children's clubs, and youth programs?	☐	☐	☐
12. Do our internal employee policies reflect a positive focus (building on strengths, etc.)?	☐	☐	☐

Youth Involvement

13. Do we actively seek ways to involve youth (through volunteering, internships, apprenticeships, or other work-readiness opportunities)?	☐	☐	☐
14. Do we enhance youth leadership skills by preparing youth for real roles and positions within our organization?	☐	☐	☐
15. Have we addressed barriers to youth participation (such as money/cost, time availability, transportation, accessibility, cultural differences, and language)?	☐	☐	☐
16. Do we publicly recognize and celebrate youth contributions?	☐	☐	☐

Community Partnerships

17. Are we familiar with other community resources to which we can refer children and families with specific needs?	☐	☐	☐
18. Do we organize with others to unite the community around asset-building strategies?	☐	☐	☐
19. Do we organize with other community leaders to advocate for public policies that support children, youth, and families?	☐	☐	☐
20. Do we provide management consulting or other expertise/services to schools and other organizations serving children and youth directly?	☐	☐	☐

After you have completed this worksheet, use it as a discussion starter. What are your current asset-building strengths? How can you build on them? What are your areas of opportunity? What things can you not do, given the structure, nature, or mission of your organization? How can this tool help you in making plans and developing ways to act?

Asset-Building Ideas and Tools for Community-Wide Initiatives

Handouts 55-65

Asset-Building **Ideas** for
Healthy Communities • Healthy Youth Teams

The seeds of a Healthy Community · Healthy Youth initiative can be planted by one committed individual, but a team working together can accomplish much more in a shorter period of time. However, working as a team can be a challenge, even when all members share a common goal. Focusing on asset building in the community as well as among team members can help keep you working effectively toward your common goal. Here are ideas on how to build assets as a team:

✿ Create a study group to explore the importance of asset building in the community.

✿ **Make time for team members to build relationships and build assets for one another.**

✿ Give people the chance to share asset-building stories at every opportunity.

✿ **Generate a mission, goals, and a logo for your initiative.**

✿ Save yourself time and effort by not re-inventing the wheel. Resources such as *Speaking of Developmental Assets* and *The Asset Activist's Toolkit* are available from Search Institute (www.search-institute.org). These provide you with much of the information and tools you need. Other excellent resources are available on networking, community development, and related topics. For ideas, contact a library, bookstore, or local community-development agency or look for information on the Web.

✿ **Link with existing community networks to help spread the word about asset building.**

✿ Learn what established organizations and programs are already doing to build assets. Acknowledge their contributions and invite them to join your team.

✿ **Go where people already gather to discuss common asset-building goals. Civic**

organizations, clergy associations, and service organizations are a few options.

✿ Distribute the asset message using creative and varied strategies, such as placing brochures in waiting rooms at clinics or printing them on grocery bags.

✿ **Publish a weekly column in your community newspaper featuring asset-building stories.**

✿ Provide literature on assets to parents of newborns and newly adoptive parents.

✿ **Sponsor or support community-wide events for families. Make sure that information about asset building and your initiative is available.**

✿ Train businesses in the asset language and encourage their participation in your initiative.

✿ **Divide the team into task forces or smaller working groups to take on particular projects or tasks.**

✿ Make connections between schools and the community through business/teacher exchanges.

✿ **Plan a career fair with local businesses. Provide all participants with information about assets and encourage them to think of the ways their organizations can build assets. Then invite youth to** talk with these potential employers about the kinds of work they do and the skills and experience needed.

❀ Bring together asset-building organizations in the community, such as 4-H, Boy Scouts, Girl Scouts, and YMCA programs. Encourage them to learn from and support one another.

❀ Identify key people in the community who could be allies in asset building and invite them to get involved with your initiative.

❀ Extend the school day by providing a community education program that includes evening and weekend learning experiences for individuals and families.

❀ Encourage service to others (asset 9) by sponsoring or supporting fund-raising projects such as paint-a-thons, bike-a-thons, and other community-wide service efforts.

❀ Supply local restaurants with table tents and place mats printed with information about asset building. Use the artwork of students to decorate them.

❀ Hold community roundtable discussions to talk about assets and encourage networking.

❀ Use asset-building language everywhere. Using the words often makes the ideas part of everyday conversation.

❀ Change the meeting place each time so that each group member can host a meeting. For example, a business executive could have the meeting one week at the executive's company, a high school student could host it another week at the high school, and a neighborhood resident could have the meeting at a neighborhood park. These changes encourage people to talk about the setting and let the host show others her or his environment.

❀ Publish a list of group members with each person's full name, address, and best way to connect (such as by phone or e-mail). Encourage people to bring the list each time. Some people will use it as a way to get to know names. Others will use it to make connections outside of the meeting.

❀ Manage personal differences and conflicts as soon as they arise. Encourage people to think about responses and actions, rather than emotions, and to try to understand the perspectives of others.

❀ With all initiative activities, efforts, and events, make sure people understand the connections to asset building.

Recruiting Volunteers
for Asset-Building Initiatives

A key to the success of an asset-building initiative is a volunteer corps that does the bulk of the work. What's true for assets is true for asset-building volunteers—the more the better. Roles for volunteers can range from creating informal relationships with youth, to joining asset-building task forces, to developing newsletters and promotional materials. Engaging volunteers and keeping them interested isn't always easy, especially with busy schedules and lots of demands on people's time. Here are some suggestions on how to get and keep volunteers for commu-nity initiatives:

GETTING VOLUNTEERS

✿ **When recruiting, include people who are sometimes overlooked as potential volunteers** because they are assumed to be too busy, not interested, or "recipients" rather than providers of service. For example, consider people who are poor, those for whom English is not their first language, single parents, working parents, newcomers to the community, developmentally disabled people, senior citizens, families, children, and youth.

✿ **Focus on the hopefulness of the assets** and the power that individuals have to make a difference for kids.

✿ **Use current volunteers as your best spokespersons** in recruiting new volunteers.

✿ **Target recruitment efforts to specific groups you want to involve.** For example, young adults might be reached effectively through athletic clubs or teams, employers, or colleges and universities; seniors might be reached through congregate dining programs, travel clubs, or community centers; volunteers of color might be reached through congregations, fraternities and sororities, and professional groups.

✿ **Make presentations to groups to find volunteers.** Parent-teacher-student organizations, high school assemblies, businesses, congregations, and youth-serving organizations are potential places to target.

✿ **Find out if a volunteer center exists in your community.** You can often find volunteers through these centers. If one doesn't exist, collaborate with other organizations that need volunteers to see if you can set one up.

✿ **Personally meet and talk with potential volunteers** on their own turf (such as in their neighborhood or work site). If that cannot be done, at least try to do recruiting face-to-face.

✿ **If you do initial recruitment by a sign-up sheet, make sure that you do a personal follow-up within a week or two.** Lack of quick action will give potential volunteers the message that you don't really want them.

✿ **If possible, have a job description for each volunteer.** Make sure that the title of the position accurately reflects the responsibilities. People are more willing to volunteer if the tasks, the time commitment, the location, the project goals, and the training requirements are all clearly stated.

✿ **When seeking volunteers, consider creating a profile of the type of people you're looking for.** List the skills, talents, and experiences you would like them to have.

✿ **See if your local newspaper has a column listing volunteer needs,** and advertise the positions you are seeking to fill.

✿ **Create easy, short-term projects for busy people** and long-term commitments for people willing to give more time and energy.

KEEPING VOLUNTEERS

✿ **Hire or recruit a volunteer coordinator.** If volunteers tire or become bored, their attendance may become more erratic. If they do not see an impact or change, they may become disillusioned and quit. A volunteer coordinator can keep in touch with volunteers and make sure their needs are met.

✿ **Remember that volunteers have different reasons for serving;** learn what motivates each one and strive to meet their needs.

✿ **Be careful not to equate volunteering for the initiative with committing to build assets.** Both are important, but they are different. Encourage all volunteers in the initiative to make a personal commitment to building assets in their personal and professional lives.

✿ **Offer opportunities for volunteers to advance** in terms of leadership, responsibility, and developing new talents and skills.

✿ **Remember that a happy volunteer will be your best recruiter** of other volunteers.

✿ **Recognize, honor, and thank volunteers.**

Involving Youth
in Your Asset-Building Initiative

Youth involvement builds assets at the same time that it strengthens the ability of an initiative to have a real and lasting impact on all young people in the community. Involving young people in planning, leading, and decision making gives an initiative a richness and authenticity that is well worth any complications that adds. (It also builds asset 8: Youth as Resources.)

Ideally, young people should be involved in asset-building initiatives from the very beginning. However, that isn't always easy to do; many adults are used to planning and leading things *for* youth rather than *with* them. The first step is making a commitment to do the work needed to get youth involved. Once you've done that, try some of these recruiting, training, and action ideas from communities that have successfully brought youth on board:

RECRUITING

- ✿ **Focus on building relationships with young people who are or might be involved in your initiative.** While it might be tempting to "get to work" right away, taking the time to get to know young people and to let them get to know you will make them more likely to want to get and stay involved.

- ✿ **Conduct a youth leadership retreat with high school students.** Train them in the asset framework. Get their ideas on how to build assets and make your community an asset-building one. At the end of the retreat, ask for volunteers for your initiative.

- ✿ **Make a list of meaningful ways to involve youth.** Then brainstorm a list of youth to involve. Contact people in schools, youth-serving organizations, congregations, service-learning programs, and neighborhood groups with names of young people to recommend. Ask about young people who may already be involved in asset building.

- ✿ **Look beyond the "usual suspects."** Reach out to youth who are not in student government, athletics, or other high-profile activities.

TRAINING

- ✿ **Conduct a training session for youth and adults on how to work effectively together.**

- ✿ **Train young people in your initiative to be peer helpers or mentors.** Suggest that they use these skills in their schools, congregations, and neighborhoods and with their friends.

❖ **Train teams or pairs of youth and adults to speak about asset building.** These teams could speak to Rotary or Lions groups, youth organizations, schools, community groups, or other groups or organizations.

❖ **Expect some adults to resist involving youth in decision-making and leadership positions.** Many adults are not used to working side by side with youth. Discuss concerns openly and look for successful ways for youth and adults to work together.

ACTION

❖ **Empower youth to come up with their own asset-building ideas.** Support them in making their ideas come to life.

❖ **Don't limit youth involvement to one special committee or task force.** Engage young people in leading and guiding your efforts, including visioning, planning, decision making, and getting the word out about asset building and the initiative.

❖ **Create a youth advisory board for your initiative.** Or designate a specific number of positions on each of your task forces, boards, and other groups for youth to hold. For example, one community initiative has a 32-member steering committee with 16 youth and 16 adult representatives.

❖ **Have both youth and adults regularly evaluate the role of young people.** Are youth really being used as resources? Or are they simply viewed as tokens or recipients of your efforts?

❖ **Be clear about young people's roles and levels of authority.** If you say they are equal partners, then treat their decisions and actions as you would treat those of an adult.

❖ **Develop specific tasks and projects for young people.** Teenagers, especially younger teens, will be better able to contribute if they have clear guidelines and goals for what to do.

❖ **So that no one starts to dominate meetings, set up a regular system for getting input from everyone.** For example, you could go around the group at each meeting and offer each participant the chance to speak.

Building Assets for
Hard-to-Reach Kids

One of the fundamental principles of asset building is that *all* children and youth need assets. Yet most people and organizations have some young people with whom they interact regularly, some with whom they interact occasionally, and others with whom they have no contact at all. Unfortunately, kids who are disconnected from one part of the community are often disconnected from most parts of the community. These "hard-to-reach" kids may be the ones most in need of asset building. There are at least two keys to building assets for hard-to-reach kids; the first is reaching out to them and the second is providing them with asset-building opportunities and relationships. Here are some ideas on how to do each:

REACHING OUT TO HARD-TO-REACH KIDS

✿ **Be truthful and sincere with young people;** tell them why you are reaching out to them and why you care.

✿ **Think about why some kids are hard to reach.** Are they staying away from you or are you staying away from them? If they are staying away from you, invite a few kids you trust to talk with you about how they think you could reach out to others. If you are choosing to work with young people with whom you are most familiar, challenge yourself to reach beyond what's comfortable for you.

✿ **Once you successfully reach out to and get to know a few young people, ask them to spread the word among their friends.** Train youth to be asset-building leaders and peer helpers.

✿ **Volunteer in an alternative school,** GED program, or program for teenage parents.

✿ **Go to places where young people hang out.** Get to know young people there.

✿ **Head to detention.** Volunteer to supervise a detention hall and befriend those who are there.

✿ **Publicize and offer free food** whenever you have some kind of youth activity. Food is often a good way to draw people in.

✿ **Volunteer at drop-in centers** and arrange to lead some constructive activities, such as a basketball game or a juggling seminar.

BUILDING ASSETS FOR HARD-TO-REACH KIDS

✿ **Be authentic.** Don't try to be something you're not because you think hard-to-reach kids will like you more. They'll figure out that you are not being yourself and then they won't trust you.

✿ **Always make time for young people** when they need or want to talk or just be with someone. Make relationship building your first priority.

✿ **Focus on drawing out young people's strengths** rather than changing what you think is wrong with them.

✿ **Work with young people to create safe places for them to spend time**—places where they feel not only physically safe but also safe to be themselves.

✿ **Find out what positive activities young people are already involved or interested in** and build on and encourage those.

✿ **Challenge young people to set goals** that are beyond what is comfortable for them, and then help them develop the skills to achieve those goals.

✿ **Learn about signs of depression, chemical abuse, eating disorders, gang involvement, and physical, sexual, or emotional abuse.** Know what resources in your community are available for kids who are struggling or in crisis. Find out who you can turn to if you feel a young person needs more help than you can offer.

✿ **Be prepared to have your goodwill and commitment tested.** Hard-to-reach kids have usually been let down by adults and might be skeptical about what you have to offer.

✿ **Give young people many opportunities to be leaders** in formal and informal ways.

✿ **Offer support groups, activities, and counseling with an explicit asset-building focus.** Train youth to lead peer support groups.

✿ **Teach young people problem-solving skills** such as using Peaceful Conflict Resolution (asset 36), Interpersonal Competence (33), and Planning and Decision Making (32).

✿ **Create opportunities for young people to make real contributions** to their communities through service projects.

✿ **Offer skill-building training for adults.** Focus on things such as Family Support (asset 1), Adult Role Models (14), and Achievement Motivation (21).

✿ **Take a positive, asset-driven approach to young people.** Instead of labeling them "at risk," think of them as having great potential.

✿ **Treat all young people with respect and care.**

✿ **Learn to trust young people** to make decisions and take responsibility.

✿ **Set, communicate, and uphold clear limits and boundaries.**

✿ **Withhold judgment,** especially about past behavior.

✿ **Offer young people opportunities** to see and experience other lifestyles and new situations.

✿ **Link hard-to-reach young people with caring, principled adults.** Train the adults beforehand so they're familiar with the 40 Developmental Assets and how to nurture them.

✿ **Be an advocate for individual young people** as well as youth in general.

Ensuring **Diversity**
in Asset-Building Efforts

Just as young people will be more successful in life if they develop a knowledge of and comfort with people of different cultural, racial, and ethnic backgrounds (asset 34), community initiatives working on behalf of asset building need to ensure that they are intentionally inclusive of *all* members of the community. It can be easier and more comfortable to assemble people who live in similar neighborhoods, share common values and beliefs, look alike, talk alike, and think alike. However, breaking down invisible walls and working together is an important part of asset building. Building these bridges increases accessible resources and opportunities, making it more likely that all kids in our communities will get the assets they need. Here are some ideas for widening your asset-building circle:

✿ **Think about how you are defining your community.** Are you using geography or a shared interest? Are you leaving any groups or neighborhoods out? Are you including people who might not think of themselves as part of your community?

✿ **Learn as much as you can about the diversity of your community.** How many languages are spoken? How many people of different age-groups live there? What's the racial and ethnic makeup of your community? Which religions are represented? What is your community's socioeconomic makeup? What is the educational makeup?

✿ **Learn more about "where people are coming from"** by listening to others talk about their perspectives and opinions; reading about specific cultural traditions, histories, current issues, and communication styles; and reflecting on your own cultural roots and how they have shaped who you are.

✿ **Always provide copies of handouts, meeting agendas, and other information and materials in as many languages as possible.** For example, you may be able to reach out to recent Somali immigrants in your community if you translate materials

and invite Somali people who speak English well to share information with others who might not otherwise be comfortable getting involved. (The list of Developmental Assets is currently available in English, Spanish, and French.)

✿ **Join or collaborate with existing cooperative efforts in your community** (such as interfaith or multicultural groups) and introduce those involved to the idea of Developmental Assets. Talk with them about the assets and look for ways to work together.

✿ **Work with human service organizations that have experience in working on cultural/racial dialogue, interfaith efforts, and other coalitions.** Implement some of their ideas to make your asset-building efforts more inclusive.

✿ **Consider adding asset building to various cultural events, holidays, and celebrations** in your community (such as New Year celebrations or high school graduations).

✿ **In addition to building diversity, also work at ways to help people build personal relationships** and have positive experiences that help them feel comfortable with people who are different from them.

✿ **Address people's prejudices and discomfort openly**.

✿ **Check to see if the people involved in partnerships are representative of the people in your community.** If not, why not?

✿ **Connect with media targeted at specific audiences.** For example, your community may have a radio station geared toward Native Americans, a newspaper that covers women's issues, or a television channel devoted to Hmong speakers.

✿ **Don't assume that people who seem to have similar characteristics see themselves as part of one group.** For example, in some communities, the term "Latino/Latina" may describe 85 percent of the community. However, individuals may identify themselves as Mexican Americans, Puerto Rican Americans, or Cuban Americans.

Modeling Assets in
Leadership Groups

While Search Institute's model of Developmental Assets is centered around the needs of youth, the basic framework can also be a useful tool for creating a healthy culture in teams leading an asset-building initiative. Equally important, using it this way reinforces and models the work you're doing to build assets in the community. Here are 16 tips linked to the eight categories of Developmental Assets that will improve the health of your leadership team:

Support

✿ **Take time in each meeting for people to connect with each other.** This may include using name tags and starting with a warm-up team-building activity.

✿ **Create a climate in the team where people feel comfortable, accepted, and connected.** If individuals seem disengaged from the group process, check with them to be sure that they do not feel alienated or ignored. If they are, work together to find ways to change that.

Empowerment

✿ **Actively involve the team members in decision making and in shaping the team efforts.** Members won't really be contributing if they are simply asked to OK plans or ideas made by others.

✿ **Make sure all group members feel valued and valuable as contributors to the team.** Know what individuals contribute as well as what group or organization they represent.

Boundaries and Expectations

✿ **Establish clear ground rules** about how the group will work together —what's expected of individual members, what strategies will be used to problem-solve, and how decisions will be made.

✿ **Clarify expectations of the roles people play in meetings.** It's a good idea to designate a facilitator, a recorder, a timekeeper, and a process observer.

Constructive Use of Time

✿ **Use people's time wisely by carefully planning meetings.** Seek input before developing an agenda, send the agenda out in advance, and be clear about the goal for each agenda item (discussion, decision, action, etc.). Start and end meetings on time.

Pass It On!
Handout 60

❉ **Respect people's time limits** by not overscheduling meetings (either in frequency or length). Keep in mind that most people lead busy lives with multiple commitments.

Commitment to Learning

❉ **Include opportunities during your meetings for learning about the community, about children and youth, and about asset building.** Not only will this enrich people's understanding, but it will strengthen the group's ability to make thoughtful decisions.

❉ **Don't assume that you always have to turn to an outside expert for knowledge.** Give team members opportunities to research issues or ideas, identify resources, and then present what they've learned to the whole group.

Positive Values

❉ **Articulate the values that guide your group's vision and deliberations.**

❉ **Develop ground rules for team process** that reflect commitments to being honest, respecting each other, and honoring commonly held values.

Social Competencies

❉ **Build team members' capabilities and skills through such practices as sharing leadership** by rotating team roles (facilitator, etc.) among members.

❉ **Nurture people's competence in working with a diverse group.** This includes training youth and adult members in working together.

Positive Identity

❉ **Develop a clear sense of the group's purpose and vision.** While you may not need a formal mission statement, it's important for people to be clear about why they are spending time together.

❉ **Celebrate together.** Celebrate the gifts of team members, the community, your accomplishments, and your hopes for the future.

Leading Successful Meetings
with Young People and Adults

Part of "walking the assets talk"—doing yourself what you tell others to do—is having both youth and adults participate in leadership and decision making. But how do you make sure this is a good experience for everyone involved?

GETTING STARTED

✿ **Be creative and sensitive about meeting times and places.** For example, if evening meeting times interfere with adults' time with their families and Saturday times are bad for Jewish youth, meet on a weekday at lunchtime in the school cafeteria. Identify group members who can offer rides to others who need them.

✿ **Understand the needs of all participants.** Offer child care if needed. Provide meeting notes for those who cannot attend.

✿ **Since many youth don't carry calendars with them, have adults make reminder phone calls** a day or two before each meeting.

✿ **If adults don't know the young people's needs, have them ask the young people** and then ask again after a meeting or two.

✿ **If youth don't know adults' needs, have them ask the adults** and then ask again after a meeting or two.

✿ **Serve snacks!**

COMMUNICATION AND LANGUAGE ISSUES

✿ **Talk openly about language issues.** Will you all go by first names? Is the term "kids" offensive to some participants? What about statements like, "You're too young to understand" or "You're too old to understand"?

✿ **Become aware of and confront your biases.** Watch for unconscious stereotyping by age, appearance or clothing style, gender, race, ethnicity, or economic class.

✿ **Give each participant—youth and adult—a chance to talk,** and give each speaker your full attention.

✿ **Talk with each other seriously** and be ready to redirect the conversation if one generation starts to talk too much, interrupt or ignore others, or be critical or scolding.

✿ **If youth are hesitant to speak up or tend to respond "I don't know" to questions they probably have an answer for, help them identify the reasons for their reticence** (e.g., fear of put-downs, difficulty telling when people are done talking). Be encouraging when young people do speak up.

TRAINING, SUPPORT, AND PROCESS

✿ **Make sure to bring new people—youth and adult—up to speed.** Review the group's goals and provide pre-meeting training for newcomers about basics such as meeting structures, discussion ground rules, and agendas and reports.

✿ **Be aware of the developmental needs of young people and accommodate the preferred learning styles of all group members.** This may mean adding more experiential meeting elements, augmenting written and verbal communications with visual aids, and breaking into small groups.

✿ **Start off with an icebreaker, game, or other fun activity** that helps participants with the transition from other activities to the meeting.

✿ **Have youth and adults periodically evaluate the role of participants.** For example, are youth being given only insignificant or peripheral tasks?

✿ **Be clear about each participant's role** and level of authority, the time and number of meetings, and the expected duration of the commitment.

✿ **Plan concrete projects.** Give youth responsibilities early, and expect achievement.

✿ **Let everyone learn from her or his own mistakes.**

✿ **Balance leadership roles** and positions between youth and adults.

Helping Adults and Kids
Build Relationships

Most of the 40 Developmental Assets are built through positive relationships. While family and peers are key, there's a third type of relationship—friendships between adults and kids who aren't related to each other—that is often overlooked as critical to development. These cross-age friendships (some people use the term "intergenerational") are key to asset building whether or not people have strong family and peer ties. They can provide both youth and adults with support, new perspectives, and sensitivity to the needs of people of different ages. Here are some suggestions for how to nurture these relationships for yourself and others:

Building Your Own Intergenerational Relationships

✿ **Make a commitment to connect and spend time with at least one person who is significantly older or younger than you are.** One resource for ideas on things to do together is Search Institute's book *Tag, You're It! 50 Easy Ways to Connect with Young People.*

Encouraging Others to Build Intergenerational Relationships

✿ **Encourage people of all ages to offer spontaneous gestures of support to one another.** These are simple, easy things to do, such as calling people by name, smiling at them, asking them about their day, and spending a few moments talking with them.

✿ **Support and encourage mentoring programs** in your community. Mentoring programs carefully match caring adults with young people and encourage them to build relationships.

✿ **Take advantage of congregations' natural intergenerational community.** Encourage congregations to plan events that include people of all ages.

✿ **Encourage and train older people in the community to view themselves and act as "elders."** Discuss the important role that older people have in the lives of young people.

✿ **Identify and celebrate people, places, and programs that connect old and young,** adults and youth, teenagers and children. Encourage others to emulate these successful intergenerational connections.

✿ **Organize intergenerational community service projects,** such as cleaning up a local park or helping at a shelter.

✿ **Find mutually beneficial ways to bring together people of many different ages** for growth and learning, such as intergenerational music or theater groups, support groups, community education classes, or walking clubs.

Planning Community-Wide
Asset-Building Events

Community-wide events are an important element of an asset-building campaign. "Community-wide" can refer to a neighborhood, school community, town, city, state, or other definition of community. These events can be used to celebrate the great things already happening in a community, raise awareness of community needs, and bring people together in a way that encourages support and relationship building. They also provide a stage to share the asset message with a wide audience. Here are a few ideas about how to successfully plan and hold community-wide asset-building events:

✿ **Develop a steering committee** that includes people who can think about the big picture of what will happen at the event as well as concrete, action-oriented people who can focus on the details of making your ideas a reality. You need both dreamers and doers.

✿ **Identify your natural partners.** The best events succeed, thanks to strong, broad-based support. Invite groups and organizations who have a common interest in youth, children, and families. They will bring vision, energy, leadership, and an existing constituency to the event.

✿ **Establish clear objectives early on.** Make sure the organizers share similar ideas about what you want to accomplish with your asset-building event.

✿ **Name your event.** Take time to come up with a name that accurately describes the event and is interesting enough to draw people's attention and enthusiasm. Be careful to avoid negative connotations or associations. One asset-building event mistakenly drew a number of people seeking information on financial investing!

✿ **Pick a date that works for as many of the organizers as possible** and doesn't conflict with religious holidays or other community events or activities.

✿ **Determine a structure for your event.** Is this part of a long-term public awareness campaign or a single event? Do you need materials, speakers, small-group facilitators? How much time can you expect people to commit?

✿ **Once you have settled on when and what you want your event to be, decide on where to hold it.** Select a place that is affordable, comfortable for and welcoming to all, in a convenient location, near easy parking, close to a bus line, and handicap-accessible.

✿ **Appoint a finance committee.** Estimate a budget and ask the committee to investigate funding sources.

✿ **Make sure you have or can get all of the audiovisual and sound equipment you need.** A sound system can make or break your event. Find someone in your group with expertise in this area and ask them to coordinate it.

✿ **Create registration forms and information sheets.**

✿ **Appoint a marketing committee and develop a marketing plan.** Determine who your primary audience is and then select the best ways to reach your audience. Options include personal invitations from organizers, mailed invitations, announcements in newspapers, and news items or ads on the radio or television. Consider sending out a press release about your event well in advance that may draw media attention before and during the event. Also consider less conventional marketing outlets, such as congregational bulletins, newsletters of local organizations, and flyers to schools, family education classes, or child-care providers.

✿ **Personally invite members of the media to your event.** Take the time to talk with them about the event's significance for your community and where it fits into your asset-building campaign. Offer to waive any fees involved. Make sure someone is assigned to help them get photos, quotes, or interviews they need. Have a designated spokesperson who can be available later that day or the next morning to answer questions as reporters put their stories together.

✿ **Decide whether or not you will include food as part of your event.** It can be a draw but can also add a lot of cost and hassle. If you plan on having food, assign the menu and timing of the food to someone who has experience. Keep in mind that entire meals can be costly and difficult to serve.

✿ **Include a satisfaction survey** as part of the event.

✿ **After the event, gather the organizers to talk about what went well, what didn't go well, and what you would do differently in the future.** Keep the comments on file in case you hold this same type of event another time.

✿ **Celebrate your success and everyone who helped make it happen.**

Honoring Asset Builders

Most people like to be recognized for good things they do. Honoring individuals and organizations that build assets not only feels good for the people honored, it also keeps the asset-building momentum going. Here are some ideas for honoring asset builders:

✿ **Choose an asset-builder-of-the-month.** One community photographs the asset builder in action and writes a press release about her or his activities. A community newspaper publishes the item and one congregation sets up a display surrounded by holiday lights that has a person's photo in the middle and a short description of her or his contributions.

✿ **Name asset-builders-of-the-year.** You may want to choose a lot of people or organizations or just a few. If you name individuals, select people of different ages.

✿ **Think of honoring asset builders as a way of inspiring others.** Be sure to share the stories of what honorees have done; they may spark others' ideas.

✿ **Have someone design thank-you bookmarks that say "Awesome Asset Builder" or "Outstanding Asset Builder."** They could include a place to list characteristics of volunteer asset builders, such as caring, thoughtful, cheerful, understanding, a good listener, and so on.

✿ **Give a "touching" appreciation.** Arrange for students from a local school of massage to come to an asset-builder appreciation event and give short massages to the asset builders. Give each person you honor an outline of a hand with an individual message of thanks inside.

✿ **Ask local businesses to donate items or services that you can give as thank-you gifts.** Items could include a gift certificate from a restaurant or store, movie tickets, a plant from a local nursery, T-shirts signed by children and youth, or free video rentals. It's good public relations for businesses to donate items to an important cause such as asset building.

✿ **Interview a child or teenager who knows the asset builder being honored.** Ask for examples and stories of what the asset builder has done for kids. Write these up and present them to the asset builder during an event.

✿ **Plan an annual tea, reception, or other recognition for honoring asset builders.** (These do not need to be costly, but they should be creative and affirming.) Consider inviting individuals whose lives were touched by the asset builders to host the event or provide treats or service.

✿ **Create an asset-builder photo wall.** Take a photograph of each person you want to honor and make a collage. Put names and a description of each person's efforts next to her or his photo. Some places have had asset builders hold their hands outstretched when taking the photos and then linked the photos hand in hand.

Asset-Building Days, Weeks, and Months
to Celebrate

There are lots of reasons to celebrate asset building every day! But here are some specific days, weeks, and months (with some possible asset connections noted) that you can use as reasons to honor and acknowledge the importance of asset building for kids in your community.

JANUARY

- **National Mentoring Month**—January (asset 3: Other Adult Relationships; 14: Adult Role Models)

- **International Creativity Month**—January (asset 17: Creative Activities)

- **National Hugging Day**—January 21 (Support assets: 1–6)

FEBRUARY

- **International Boost Self-Esteem Month**—February (asset 38: Self-Esteem)

- **Black History Month**—February (asset 34: Cultural Competence)

- **Pay-a-Compliment Day**—February 6 (Support and Empowerment assets: 1–10; asset 26: Caring)

- **International Friendship Week**—Last full week in February (asset 33: Interpersonal Competence)

MARCH

- **Youth Art Month**—March (asset 17: Creative Activities)

- **I Want You to Be Happy Day**—March 3 (Support assets: 1–6; asset 26: Caring)

- **Good Samaritan Involvement Day**—March 13 (asset 9: Service to Others; Positive-Identity assets: 37–40; asset 26: Caring; 27: Equality and Social Justice; 38: Self-Esteem)

APRIL

- **Thank You School Librarian Day**—April 5 (asset 3: Other Adult Relationships; 14: Adult Role Models; 25: Reading for Pleasure)

- **Week of the Young Child**—Usually in April, but dates vary from year to year (children's assets 1–40)

- **National Youth Service Days**—The third weekend (Friday–Sunday) in April (asset 7: Community Values Youth; 8: Youth as Resources; 9: Service to Others; Positive-Values assets: 26–31)

- **National Volunteer Week**—Usually in April, but dates vary from year to year (9: Service to Others; Positive-Values assets: 26-31)

- **National Playground Safety Week**—Usually the fourth week in April (asset 10: Safety)

- **National Honesty Day**—April 30 (asset 29: Honesty)

MAY

- **National Physical Fitness and Sports Month—**May (asset 18: Youth Programs)

- **School Principal's Day—**May 1 (asset 3: Other Adult Relationships; 14: Adult Role Models; Commitment-to-Learning assets: 21–25)

- **Teacher Appreciation Week—**First full week in May (Support and Commitment-to-Learning assets: 1–6 and 21–25; asset 14: Adult Role Models)

- **National Family Week—**First full week in May (asset 1: Family Support)

- **Reading Is Fun Week—**Usually the third week in May (asset 22: School Engagement; 25: Reading for Pleasure)

- **Mother's Day—**Second Sunday in May (asset 1: Family Support; 14: Adult Role Models)

JUNE

- **Student Safety Month—**June (asset 10: Safety)

- **International Volunteers Week—**First seven days in June (9: Service to Others; Positive-Values assets: 26–31)

- **Race Unity Day—**Second Sunday in June (asset 34: Cultural Competence)

- **Father's Day—**Third Sunday in June (asset 1: Family Support; 14: Adult Role Models)

JULY

- **Family Reunion Month—**July (asset 1: Family Support; 2: Positive Family Communication)

- **National Purposeful Parenting Month—**July (assets 1–40)

- **National Recreation and Parks Month—**July (asset 17: Creative Activities; 18: Youth Programs)

- **Social Wellness Month—**July (Social-Competencies assets: 32-36)

AUGUST

- **Be Kind to Humankind Week—**Last week of August (asset 26: Caring; 27: Equality and Social Justice)

- **The Date to Create (promotes crativity and innovation)—**August 8 (asset 17: Creative Activities)

SEPTEMBER

- **Self-Improvement Month** (to celebrate the importance of lifelong learning and self-improvement)—September (Commitment-to-Learning, Positive-Values, Social-Competencies, and Positive-Identity assets: 21–40)

- **Baby Safety Month—**September (asset 7: Community Values Youth; 10: Safety)

- **National Grandparents Day—**First Sunday in September following Labor Day (asset 1: Family Support; 3: Other Adult Relationships; 14: Adult Role Models)

- **National Good Neighbor Day—**Fourth Sunday in September (asset 4: Caring Neighborhood; 13: Neighborhood Boundaries; 14: Adult Role Models)

OCTOBER

- **National Book Month**—October (asset 25: Reading for Pleasure)

- **Diversity Awareness Month**—October (asset 34: Cultural Competence)

- **National Communicate with Your Kid Month**—October (asset 1: Family Support; 2: Positive Family Communication)

- **World Smile Day**—First Friday in October (Support assets: 1–6)

- **YWCA Week Without Violence**—Third full week in October (asset 26: Caring; 35: Resistance Skills; 36: Peaceful Conflict Resolution)

- **Make a Difference Day** (a national day of community service)—Fourth Saturday in October (asset 8: Youth as Resources; 9: Service to Others; 26: Caring; 27: Equality and Social Justice)

- **Peace, Friendship, and Good Will Week**—Last seven days of October (asset 26: Caring; 27: Equality and Social Justice; 33: Interpersonal Competence; 34: Cultural Competence; 36: Peaceful Conflict Resolution)

NOVEMBER

- **National Children's Book Week**—Second or third week in November (asset 25: Reading for Pleasure)

- **American Education Week**—First full week preceding the fourth Thursday in November (Commitment-to-Learning assets: 21–25)

- **National Young Readers Day**—Varies from year to year (asset 25: Reading for Pleasure)

- **Universal Children's Day**—November 20 (assets 1–40)

- **National Family Volunteer Day**—Saturday before Thanksgiving (asset 8: Youth as Resources; 9: Service to Others; 26: Caring; 27: Equality and Social Justice)

DECEMBER

- **Universal Human Rights Month**—December (Positive-Values assets: 26–31; 34: Cultural Competence; Positive-Identity assets: 37–40)

- **World Peace Day**—Winter Solstice: December 21 or 22 (asset 26: Caring; 27: Equality and Social Justice; 34: Cultural Competence; 36: Peaceful Conflict Resolution)

- **Make Up Your Mind Day**—December 31 (asset 32: Planning and Decision Making)

Source: Chase's 2006 Calendar of Events *(published annually by McGraw-Hill)*

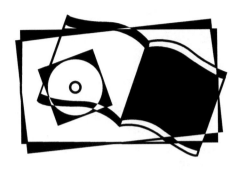

Part 5

Using Books, Movies, and Other Resources to Explore Asset-Building Themes

Handouts 66-78

Asset-Building Resources
for Individuals

When some people first hear about asset building for youth, they don't think there is much they can do because they aren't parents, teachers, aunts, or uncles. In other words, they don't have a lot of contact with kids so they don't see what they can do. But that is what is great about asset building—everyone can do it—even young people themselves. Once people start learning about what they can do to build assets, they usually don't want to stop. Here are some resources for understanding the power of the assets for young people and how both adults and youth can build them:

For Adults

♥ *150 Ways to Show Kids You Care/Los Niños Importan: 150 Maneras de Demostrárselo*—This warm, inviting, and colorful book provides adults easy ideas and meaningful reminders about how they can show kids they really care. Based on the best-selling poster of the same name. Includes an introduction to the Developmental Assets and 150 ideas in both English and Spanish.

♥ *The Asset Approach*—This eight-page booklet provides a perfect overview of the asset-building approach. It features the most recent Search Institute statistics, a list of the 40 Developmental Assets, an asset-building activity inspired by young people, stories of assets in action from communities, and more. (Available in English or Spanish.)

♥ *Conversations on the Go*—Looking for a fun way to start conversations with a young person? *Conversations on the Go* is bound to get you talking. The book is filled with intriguing questions, guaranteed to stretch the imagination and bring out each other's personality and true self.

♥ *Just When I Needed You: True Stories of Adults Who Made a Difference in the Lives of Young People*—This heartwarming collection of stories inspires us all to remember who was there for us as we were growing up. Adult asset champions tell stories of who encouraged them—so much so that they now intentionally build assets and make a difference for kids in their own lives. Their stories are inspiring and instructive.

♥ *Playful Reading: Positive, Fun Ways to Build the Bond between Preschoolers, Books, and You*—This book takes readers on a joyful romp through 40 asset-rich preschool-level books, linking early literacy skills and asset building. Emphasizing reading for pleasure, it includes suggestions for fun activities and discussions. The ideas in this book are based on research on how to raise children who love to read.

♥ *Stay Close: 40 Clever Ways to Connect with Kids When You're Apart*—This easy-to-read book offers adults fun and creative solutions for nurturing long-distance relationships with kids. Whether you're a grandparent, aunt, uncle, parent, or friend of a young person who lives far away, you'll

find activities, real-life anecdotes, and helpful tips to help you bridge the physical (and generational) gap.

♥ *Tag, You're It! 50 Easy Ways to Connect with Young People*—This delightful book provides 50 simple acts of caring to reach out to those young people who will thrive from the attention of a caring adult.

♥ *What Kids Need to Succeed*—Learn about the 40 Developmental Assets with this book that includes more than 900 practical ways to build assets, including specific ideas for families.

♥ *Who, Me? Surprisingly Doable Ways You Can Make a Difference for Kids*—Use this desktop perpetual calendar for reminders, tips, and inspiration in your daily interactions with kids and teens.

For Young People

♥ *Life Freaks Me Out: And Then I Deal with It*—This down-to-earth memoir touches on hard-hitting issues—drugs, alcohol, self-esteem, relationships, sex—to emphasize to today's teens the power of choice and the importance of finding their own values and truths as they grow up.

♥ *Me@My Best: Ideas for Staying True to Yourself—Every Day*—This 16-page booklet is designed specifically to introduce Developmental Assets to young people. This booklet was inspired by the voices of many young people throughout North America who know assets and how to communicate the power of "keeping it real" to their peers. The booklet introduces the framework in a youth-friendly way, encourages them to explore what the categories mean to them personally, and inspires them to find and build upon their own strengths.

♥ *Take It to the Next Level: Making Your Life What You Want it to Be*—Created just for teens and young adolescents, this book helps young people focus on their successes, explore what they really want and how to get it, and celebrate their efforts and accomplishments. Filled with activities and journal topics, this booklet guides young people through the journey of adolescence from a Developmental Asset approach.

♥ *What Teens Need to Succeed*—This book focuses on how young people can shape the future by building their own assets and those of their peers.

"Adding Assets" Series:

♥ *People Who Care About You*—Book 1 in the "Adding Assets" Series for Kids introduces and describes the six Support assets: Family Support, Positive Family Communication, Other Adult Relationships, Caring Neighborhood, Caring School Climate, and Parent Involvement in Schooling. Each asset is clearly defined and introduced by a story. Kids learn concrete, realistic ways to build family closeness and strengthen other important relationships in their lives.

♥ *Helping Out and Staying Safe*—Book 2 in the "Adding Assets" Series for Kids introduces and describes the four Empowerment assets: Community Values Children, Children as Resources, Service to Others,

and Safety. Each asset is clearly defined and introduced by a story. Kids learn simple, everyday ways to play useful roles at home and in the community, help others, and feel safer at home, at school, and in their neighborhood.

♥ *Doing and Being Your Best*—In Book 3 of the "Adding Assets" Series, kids learn how to build the six Boundaries-and-Expectations assets: Family Boundaries, School Boundaries, Neighborhood Boundaries, Adult Role Models, Positive Peer Influence, and High Expectations. Stories, tips, and ideas show them why and how boundaries help them behave in positive, responsible ways.

♥ *Smart Ways to Spend Your Time*—In Book 4 of the "Adding Assets" Series, kids learn how to build the four Constructive-Use-of-Time assets: Creative Activities, Child Programs, Religious Community, and Time at Home. Stories, tips, and ideas promote healthy, constructive, relationship-strengthening interests and activities.

All of the above resources and more are available from Search Institute: www.searchinstitutestore.org, 877-240-7251, ext. 1.

Asset-Building Resources
for Parents and Guardians

As a parent or guardian, you can and should be the most influential asset builder in your child's life. It doesn't matter if your child is an infant or a teenager, it's never too late to start building the foundation he or she needs to succeed. The resources below can help you better understand the power of the assets and give you practical parenting tips and ideas.

♥ *Ask Me Where I'm Going & Other Revealing Messages from Today's Teens*—This intimate little book will touch your heart as you read poignant and practical real words from teens describing what they really want from their parents and other caring adults in their lives. *"Let me share my worries with you ... Never give up on me ... Encourage me more, criticize me less."* This will give you some simple ideas on how to better relate to your teen.

♥ *Connect 5: Finding the Caring Adults You May Not Realize Your Teen Needs*—This book provides hope, encouragement, and practical advice for parents to reach out and help their teens connect with other responsible and supportive adults, a critical factor in their healthy development.

♥ *Conversations on the Go*—Looking for a fun way to start conversations with a young person? *Conversations on the Go* is bound to get you talking. The book is filled with intriguing questions, guaranteed to stretch the imagination and bring out each other's personality and true self.

♥ *Parenting at the Speed of Teens: Positive Tips on Everyday Issues*—This practical, easy-to-use guide offers positive, commonsense strategies for dealing with both the everyday issues of parenting teenagers (junk food, the Internet, stress, friends), as well as the more serious issues teens may encounter (depression, divorce, racism, substance abuse). Parents will find reassurance in the asset-building parenting perspective and advice.

♥ *Parenting Preschoolers with a Purpose: Caring for Your Kids and Yourself*—An easy-to-read book full of tips and strategies for dealing with the myriad challenges that go along with parenting children ages 3 to 5. It also includes lots of great ideas for making sure you continue to take care of yourself along the way.

♥ *Playful Reading: Positive, Fun Ways to Build the Bond between Preschoolers, Books, and You*—This book takes readers on a joyful romp through 40 asset-rich preschool-level books, linking early literacy skills

and asset building. Emphasizing reading for pleasure, it includes suggestion for fun activities and discussions. The ideas in this book are based on research on how to raise children who love to read.

♥ *What Kids Need to Succeed*—Learn about the 40 Developmental Assets with this book that includes more than 900 practical and specific ways to build assets, including specific ideas for families.

All of the above resources and more are available from Search Institute: www.searchinstitutestore.org, 877-240-7251, ext. 1.

Asset-Building Resources
for Educators

Integrating asset building into education is key to bringing out the best in young people. Young people with a strong foundation of assets are more likely to be engaged in learning and school. You can strengthen your own asset-building power by learning more about the assets in each of the eight categories and how to nurture them in students. Here are some resources for more information:

♥ *Bring It On Home: Connecting Parents, Kids, and Teachers*—This unique set of worksheets gives teachers a tool they can use to encourage asset building between elementary-age students and students' parents or other caring adults. Each worksheet offers several positive ideas, with sections encouraging students and parents to *"Think about It," "Talk about It,"* and *"Do Something about It."*

♥ *Building Assets Is Elementary: Group Activities for Helping Kids Ages 8–12 Succeed*—This book offers 61 fun ways to provide the guidance, wisdom, and asset-building skills that children of this age need. The activities are flexible and easily adaptable to any classroom or group setting.

♥ *Connecting in Your Classroom*—Inspirational profiles of 18 amazing teachers who are asset builders. Their stories, strategies, and secrets reveal how fostering healthy, thriving relationships helps students succeed socially and emotionally as well as academically.

♥ *Great Places to Learn, Second Edition*—Recently updated, this foundational book shines as a powerful, positive guide to infusing assets into any school community. This resource is rooted in many years of research that prove the effectiveness of assets. Readers discover real-life examples of how many schools have discovered how to restore their school communities using the assets framework.

♥ *Ideas for Parents* Newsletter Set, CD-ROM—This popular set of newsletter masters allows you to communicate with parents, introduce the assets each week for a full calendar year, and give ideas and tips to put to use right away. Thousands of schools, communities, and organizations have used them to customize, copy, and distribute to parents. The master set also includes a User's Guide with suggestions for customizing and distributing the series.

♥ *Powerful Teaching: Developmental Assets in Curriculum and Instruction*—This resource deals exclusively with the core of everyday classroom teaching and learning. It shows teachers how to infuse the assets

into their existing curriculum and instruction without starting a new program.

♥ *A Quick-Start Guide to Building Assets in Your School*—As educators are expected to do more with less these days, this book is here to help them do just that: have more positive impact on students with less effort. It offers school-wide strategies to get parents, students, and other school staff involved in creating caring classrooms.

♥ *You Have to Live It*—Winner of The Association of Educational Publishers' 2000 Distinguished Achievement Award, this video lets you see and hear for yourself how schools around North America are building assets for and with students from elementary to the high school level.

♥ *Your Classroom: Simple Ways to Create a Positive Learning Climate*— This 24-page booklet introduces the Developmental Assets and encourages teachers to foster all eight of the asset categories in their students through day-to-day interactions. It comes in packs of 20, so every teacher in a school can have one handy.

All of the above resources and more are available from Search Institute: www.searchinstitutestore.org, 877-240-7251, ext. 1.

Asset-Building Resources
for Faith-Based Organizations

One way to tap faith communities' unique asset-building potential is to educate as many people as possible about the importance of assets. Create a library of asset-building resources that can give your members new ideas and insights into how to build assets in your faith community. Here are a few resources to get you started:

♥ *Building Assets in Congregations: A Practical Guide for Helping Youth Grow Up Healthy*—This in-depth guide offers everything you'll need to create an asset-building congregation, including ideas, tips, and reproducible bulletin inserts. Perfect for youth workers, clergy, volunteers, and others.

♥ *Building Assets, Strengthening Faith: An Intergenerational Survey for Congregations*—This Web-based survey allows congregations to find out how they are doing in nurturing faith and building assets in children, youth, and families. The survey asks congregation members their perceptions of the congregation, its priorities, its growth, and how it is making a difference in the broader community.

♥ *The Handbook of Spiritual Development in Childhood and Adolescence*—This book breaks new ground by articulating the state of knowledge in the area of childhood and adolescent spiritual development. Featuring a rich array of theory and research from an international assortment of leading social scientists in multiple disciplines, this book represents work from diverse traditions and approaches—making it an invaluable resource for scholars across a variety of disciplines and organizations.

♥ *Integrating Assets into Congregations: A Curriculum for Trainers*—With this in-depth training curriculum, trainers can help teams from congregations integrate asset building throughout the congregation to strengthen their work with youth and families. This ready-to-use curriculum features flexible three-hour modules to meet the scheduling and learning needs of participants from all faiths.

All of the above resources and more are available from Search Institute: www.searchinstitutestore.org, 877-240-7251, ext. 1.

Reading **Tips**
for Infants and Toddlers (Ages Birth to 2)

Raising a reader begins years before a child learns to read independently, and even before a toddler mimics words, remembers characters, or asks to hear favorite stories repeatedly. Groundbreaking findings point to the important role that daily read-aloud times with parents and other caring adults play in early brain development. Savoring a book in your company can be as great a motivator as the book itself. Here are research-based tips for getting infants and toddlers off to a great start with reading:

From the time your baby is born, introduce nursery rhymes, songs, and finger plays as well as books with simple illustrations and engaging text. These offer an opportunity to build vocabulary and the ability to distinguish between sounds (phonological awareness)—two qualities important to later reading skills.

Give your child hands-on experiences with sturdy board books. Your child can practice simple motor skills and begin to learn how to use a book (positioning a book right-side up, turning pages from front to back, etc.) as early as 8 months of age.

Spend a total of 15 minutes per day with baby and books. Read a little bit at different times during the day. Observe baby's readiness to engage in books and laptime. Create regular reading times, such as at bedtime, after naps, or in transition from child care to home. Read with dramatic expression and enthusiasm.

Choose attention-getting books with rhyming words, repeated phrases, recurring patterns, and sounds (such as *moo, cluck,* and *boom!*).

Encourage simple discussions once your toddler has a vocabulary of 50 words. Point out and talk about content. Frequently ask "what" questions, such as "What's that?" "What color is it?" "What is she doing?" Provide answers if the child doesn't respond.

Praise a toddler's responses and spontaneous comments. Model and praise gentle use of books. Give daily affirmations about behavior and personality. Research shows that this contributes to a child's later ability to read.

Make sure your toddler comes to associate daily reading time with positive, playful experiences and one-to-one attention from you and other caring adults.

Reading **Tips**
for Children Ages 3 to 5

The preschool stage is a great time to use books to introduce a child to the wider world. Along with books that reflect specific assets, choose the best of picture books that include simple folk tales, everyday challenges, and absurd situations. Children in this age group typically enjoy silly characters; scary-but-safe story lines with predictable, happy endings; and animal tales. Be sure to share alphabet, counting, and other concept books. Here are research-based tips for helping preschoolers get the most out of reading:

Read to your child for 15 to 30 minutes daily. Borrow or buy books to ensure you expose your child to a variety of recommended, age-appropriate books. Be aware of your child's preferences.

Take your child to the public library. Spend time browsing and also attend story times and other structured activities your library may offer.

Give books as gifts on special occasions. Inscribe each book with a message that records a special event in your child's life, such as riding a bicycle with training wheels for the first time or losing her or his first tooth. In this way, you'll celebrate both book ownership and your child's own unique history.

Use books to introduce your child to people of different ages, races, genders, nationalities, and abilities.

Talk about the book before and after reading. Predict together what's to come. Explore the meaning of words and characters' actions. Initiate fun activities that bridge a story to the real world.

Link a story to your child's own experiences. Share some stories that deal with issues your child is facing in her or his own life, such as a new sibling, starting school, or fear of the dark.

Read with expression. Use different voices and facial expressions. Focus on fun!

Reading **Tips**

for Children Ages **5** to **9**

For most children ages 5 to 9, reading is hard work. While they need support and encouragement, they don't need pressure to read more or harder books. If you feel your child is lagging behind readers of the same age, you may want to seek individualized attention for her or him. At home, use these ideas to help nurture a love of reading:

Read with your child for 15 to 30 minutes daily. Children appreciate and understand far more than they can read themselves at this stage; vocabulary growth is crucial for reading success.

Make reading times special. Relax, snuggle, and laugh while you read with your child. Read with dramatic expression. Talk about what you're reading before and after diving into a poetry book, picture book, or chapter book.

Borrow and buy a variety of recommended books. Teach children to handle books with care. Give them as gifts. These acts send the message that reading is a treasured, essential part of life.

Model the importance of reading for pleasure. Hang out together at the public library. Let your children see you reading all types of literature, including books, magazines, and newspapers.

Find books that deal with issues that your child is facing in his or her own life. Examples include making new friends, taking appropriate risks, or practicing honesty. Choose some books that focus on successfully solving problems.

Use books to introduce people of different ages, races, nationalities, genders, and abilities.

Extend some readings to active play and fun activities that relate to the book you've just shared. This will deepen your child's understanding of words, concepts, and characters' experiences. It makes books come alive for your child.

Honor your child's preferences. At the same time, try to expand her or his interests by introducing a variety of books—wordless books, animal stories, counting and alphabet books, poetry, concept and information books, and stories about friendship, families, and familiar things.

Reading **Tips**
for Children Ages 9 to 12

Reading can be a great asset-building activity for people of all ages. It not only builds asset 25: Reading for Pleasure, but the right books can contribute to the development of many other assets, including 1: Family Support; 3: Other Adult Relationships; 6: Parent Involvement in Schooling; 14: Adult Role Models; 15: Positive Peer Influence; 20: Time at Home; 21: Achievement Motivation; 22: Learning Engagement; 26–31: the Positive-Values assets; 32–36: the Social-Competencies assets; 39: Sense of Purpose; and 40: Positive View of Personal Future.

Make it easy for children in the intermediate grades (4th to 6th) to get their hands on books that reflect their abilities and interests. Don't banish the picture books—they are old friends that remind young readers of their progress and prowess and provide food for thought in one satisfying sitting. If you want to raise a lifelong reader, encourage reading that is fun and satisfying. Here are some tips for helping children in the intermediate grades get the most out of reading:

Turn off the TV. Establishing a TV-free time of day or limiting TV watching will pay great dividends, since TV is the biggest distraction from active engagement with books *and* life. Limit other "screen time" (e.g., video and computer games) as well.

Make books and reading a family priority.

Read aloud together as a family. More and more activities will compete for time and attention as youth get older. Remember that reading together provides access to more difficult books, prompts discussions, and adds to closeness.

Encourage teachers to read aloud to students every day. Also advocate for regular silent reading times. Ask for summer reading lists. Encourage your child's school to stock classrooms with recreational reading material.

Spend time at a library just hanging out. Watch what kinds of books your child gravitates toward.

Model the importance of reading for pleasure by subscribing to magazines and newspapers or regularly checking out books from a library.

Honor your child's preferences and also introduce new books, such as series books, mysteries, humorous stories, fantasies, nonfiction, stories with happy endings, poetry, and books that help young people puzzle over everyday and real-world issues.

Reading **Tips**

for Young People Ages 12 to 18

Reading can be a great asset-building activity for people of all ages. It not only builds asset 25: Reading for Pleasure, but the right books can contribute to the development of many other assets, including 1: Family Support; 3: Other Adult Relationships; 6: Parent Involvement in Schooling; 14: Adult Role Models; 15: Positive Peer Influence; 20: Time at Home; 21: Achievement Motivation; 22: School Engagement; 26–31: the Positive-Values assets; 32–36: the Social-Competencies assets; 39: Sense of Purpose; and 40: Positive View of Personal Future.

The interests and insights of two 14-year-olds, not to mention a 13-year-old and a 16-year-old, can be radically different. Some feel ready to read adult books; others avoid reading altogether. Do your best to influence and inspire rather than control what your child reads. Your example, your enthusiasm, and your past efforts to raise a lifelong reader will serve you best in promoting and preserving the reading habit. Here are some tips for helping teenagers get the most out of reading:

Create a reading-friendly environment. Leave irresistible books and magazines in conspicuous places—the bathroom, bedroom, den, or car.

Turn off the TV. TV is the biggest distraction from active engagement with books *and* life. Limit other "screen time" (e.g., video and computer games) as well.

Make reading a family priority. Set aside regular individual or family reading times.

Give books as gifts on special occasions. Use books to commemorate accomplishments, wins, birthdays, holidays, or rites of passage.

Know your reader! Subscribe to a magazine that reflects your teen's interest in music, sports, cars, pop culture, or other topic. Provide books with stories or themes similar to ones your teenager has enjoyed in the recent past.

Seek out lists of recommended young adult (YA) titles. The American Library Association, for example, publishes lists of popular YA titles with fine writing, favorite authors, and themes of great interest to readers of this age-group.

Create opportunities to read aloud. Excerpts from books, riveting poems, or readings of family members' own writing all add memories and a shared frame of reference.

Keep new books coming. Look for biographies (with true tales of individuals' struggles to prevail and find their path), humor, poetry, nonfiction, realistic fiction, science fiction and fantasy, books about growing up, and books that inspire new ways of seeing/knowing/relating.

Trust your teenager's choices. Some teen fiction may have objectionable language, frank subject matter, frightening plots, or banal story lines. Talk with your teenager if you have concerns, listen to understand your teenager's point of view, but in most cases, let her or him decide what to read.

Magazines and Newsletters
with Asset-Building Themes

Periodicals can be a regular source of asset-building articles and ideas. These publications don't all use the language of assets, but they focus on themes, ideas, and values that are part of the asset approach:

Daughters Newsletter—Published by the national education and advocacy nonprofit organization, Dads and Daughters (DADs), this bimonthly newsletter offers effective parenting and communication techniques for parents of adolescent girls. Since 1999, DADs has provided tools to strengthen parent–daughter relationships and to transform the pervasive messages that value daughters more for how they look than who they are. Contact: *Daughters,* 2 West First Street, #101, Duluth, MN 55802; 888-849-8476; www.daughters.com.

Everyday Parenting Ideas—A free weekly e-mail newsletter that gives parents practical tips for building assets and enriching their relationships with their children. Published by Search Institute. To subscribe, go to www.mvparents.com. Contact: Search Institute, 615 First Avenue Northeast, Suite 125, Minneapolis, MN 55413.

National Geographic Kids—The mission of this monthly magazine is to entertain children while educating and exciting them about their world. It is a photo-driven magazine, geared toward ages 6 to 12, from the publishers of *National Geographic.* Contact: *National Geographic Kids,* P.O. Box 63002, Tampa, FL 33663-3002; 800-647-5463; www.nationalgeographic.com/kids.

New Moon: The Magazine for Girls and Their Dreams—This bimonthly magazine celebrates girls and the passage from being a girl to being a woman. It is edited by and for girls ages 8 to 14. Contact: *New Moon,* 2 West First Street, #101, Duluth, MN 55802; 800-381-4743; www.newmoon.org.

Skipping Stones Magazine—This nonprofit children's magazine encourages cooperation, creativity, and celebration of cultural and environmental richness. It provides a playful forum for sharing ideas and experiences among children from different lands and backgrounds. This educational resource publishes bimonthly from September to May each year. Contact: *Skipping Stones,* P.O. Box 3939, Eugene, OR 97403; 541-342-4956; www.skippingstones.org.

Time for Kids—From the publisher of *Time* news magazine, *Time for Kids* comes in three versions for three different age groups ranging from kindergarten to seventh grade. It covers news from around the world and includes articles on people and places of interest to kids. Contact: *Time for Kids,* 1271 Sixth Avenue, 22nd floor, New York, NY 10020; 800-777-8600; www.timeforkids.com.

Who Cares—This bimonthly, free magazine focuses on social change. It aims to be a leading resource for current and emerging community leaders. Contact: *Who Cares,* 1436 U Street, Northwest, Suite 201, Washington, DC 20009; 202-588-8920; www.whocares.org.

Wingspread Journal—Published quarterly, this free journal focuses on encouraging involvement of adults in the lives of children and youth in addition to fostering sustainable community development. Contact: *Wingspread Journal,* 33 East Four Mile Road, Racine, WI 53402; 262-639-3211; www.johnsonfdn.org.

Finding Asset-Building Books
for Kids

Young people are more likely to read if they have great books to choose from. Good reading material is one of the best educational investments a parent can make. Fortunately, libraries, book stores, and other sources offer an enormous range of choices. Here are things to keep in mind about where to find books for kids and how to choose them:

Where to Find Books for Kids

Make a trip to the library part of your regular routine.

Look for books at garage sales, rummage sales, and second-hand stores. Sometimes families will sell all of their children's books at once.

Find out if there is a used-book exchange in your neighborhood. These resale stores can be great places to find inexpensive books as well as recycle some of your own.

Check whether your community has an early childhood education program; they may have a "lending library" as part of their services.

Trade books with other families with children about your children's ages.

Shop at a children's bookstore. Ask your local bookseller about what's hot in children's literature.

Get on the mailing list for a reputable catalog. Chinaberry provides in-depth profiles of every featured book. Books are grouped by maturity level from infancy through the teen years. You can order through the catalog or their Web site. For more information, go to www.chinaberry.com.

Surf the Internet. For example, The Children's Book Council has a helpful Web site (www.cbcbooks.org) with features such as "75 Authors and Illustrators Everyone Should Know," "Not Just for Children Anymore" (citing picture books for older readers and adults), and "Children's Choices" (an annual review of books chosen by thousands of U.S. school children).

How to Choose Books for Kids

Choose books with female and male characters of different races, genders, cultures, or abilities as one way to introduce children to the multicultural society in which they live.

Look for art. Give children books that are works of beauty.

Look for books that play with language using rhythm, repetition, rhyme, and memorable phrases that are fun to read over and over again.

Do not equate the number of words with quality or value. Simple yet powerful writing such as in James Marshall's *George and Martha: The Complete Stories of Two Best Friends* (Houghton Mifflin, 1997) can be short on text but long on wisdom. Similarly, a wordless book like *ZOOM* by Istvan Banyai (Puffin Books, 1995) appeals to people of all ages.

When choosing books, concentrate on the interests and maturity level of a *specific* child or class rather than basing your selection on age. In a first-grade classroom alone, reading levels

can span six or more years. **Not every 40-year-old likes books on golf or angels. Likewise, not every 6-year-old cares about dinosaurs or riddles. Even a book that deserved its prestigious award will not appeal to everyone.**

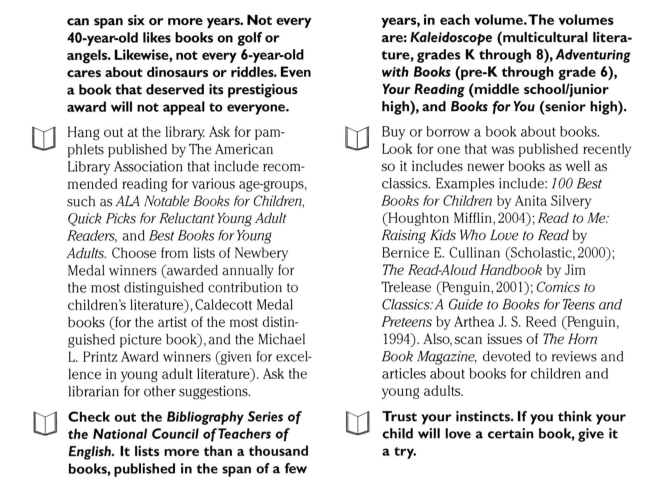

Hang out at the library. Ask for pamphlets published by The American Library Association that include recommended reading for various age-groups, such as *ALA Notable Books for Children, Quick Picks for Reluctant Young Adult Readers,* and *Best Books for Young Adults.* Choose from lists of Newbery Medal winners (awarded annually for the most distinguished contribution to children's literature), Caldecott Medal books (for the artist of the most distinguished picture book), and the Michael L. Printz Award winners (given for excellence in young adult literature). Ask the librarian for other suggestions.

Check out the *Bibliography Series of the National Council of Teachers of English.* It lists more than a thousand books, published in the span of a few

years, in each volume. The volumes are: *Kaleidoscope* (multicultural literature, grades K through 8), *Adventuring with Books* (pre-K through grade 6), *Your Reading* (middle school/junior high), and *Books for You* (senior high).

Buy or borrow a book about books. Look for one that was published recently so it includes newer books as well as classics. Examples include: *100 Best Books for Children* by Anita Silvery (Houghton Mifflin, 2004); *Read to Me: Raising Kids Who Love to Read* by Bernice E. Cullinan (Scholastic, 2000); *The Read-Aloud Handbook* by Jim Trelease (Penguin, 2001); *Comics to Classics: A Guide to Books for Teens and Preteens* by Arthea J. S. Reed (Penguin, 1994). Also, scan issues of *The Horn Book Magazine,* devoted to reviews and articles about books for children and young adults.

Trust your instincts. If you think your child will love a certain book, give it a try.

Web Sites
with Asset-Building Themes

You can learn more about asset building and each of the eight asset categories by surfing the Web. Some Web sites have practical information. Others have resources. Many have suggestions of other Web sites to visit. Keep in mind that Web sites can change without notice; the sites below were accurate at the time of this printing, but you should confirm the accuracy of each URL before sharing this handout with others.

ASSET BUILDING IN GENERAL

♥ **www.search-institute.org**—This site is filled with asset-building stories, ideas, and resources for individuals, organizations, and communities interested in asset building.

♥ **MVParents.com**—A resource developed by the Search Institute specifically for busy, caring parents who want information they can trust about raising responsible children and teens.

♥ **www.connectforkids.org**—A site with articles and information about helping children, with a special emphasis on children in low-income families. It includes asset-building information.

Support

♥ **www.mentoring.org**—The National Mentoring Partnership in Washington, D.C., provides resources for mentors and mentoring initiatives through this Web site.

♥ **www.ed.gov/parents**—The U.S. Department of Education offers information on family involvement in learning through this Web site.

Empowerment

♥ **www.ncpc.org**—The National Crime Prevention Council (NCPC), the home of McGruff the Crime Dog, publishes information and quizzes on safety and crime prevention. Check out this site to find out more about what you can do to keep kids safe.

♥ **www.youthone.com/volunteer**—A place where young people can find information about and opportunities for volunteering.

Boundaries and Expectations

♥ **www.rolemodel.net**—It is the mission of RoleModel.net to present positive role models to inspire young people to live a life that is more outward focused than inward focused.

Constructive Use of Time

♥ **www.nga.gov/kids**—National Gallery of Arts' Kids Page exists to teach children an appreciation for art.

♥ **www.fitness.gov**—This is the health, physical activity, fitness, and sports information Web site of the President's Council on Physical Fitness and Sports. You can find out about the Council and its work, view its publications, and link to the resources of other government agencies as well as to health and fitness organizations.

♥ **www.childrensmusic.org**—Children's Music Web includes music resources for performers, teachers, parents, and kids.

♥ **www.artsedge.kennedy-center.org**—Some pages in this Web site are created by students. The site also has information and resources about supporting the arts in school.

Commitment to Learning

♥ **www.cbcbooks.org**—The Children's Book Council features books, articles, and helpful information about reading for pleasure. It also publishes an annual review, called "Children's Choices" in conjunction with the International Reading Association.

♥ **www.eduplace.com**—Resources for teachers, parents, and kids. Includes kids' games and activities for math, reading, language arts, social studies, and more. This site was developed by Houghton-Mifflin publishers.

Positive Values

♥ **www.giraffe.org**—The Giraffe Heroes Project honors people who "stick their necks out" for the common good.

♥ **www.charactercounts.org**—The organization Character Counts! has identified "Six Pillars of Character," which it highlights through this Web site.

Social Competencies

♥ **www.womenswork.org/girls**—This Web site shows that girls are competent to be and do almost anything. It has a role model registry in addition to references and resources.

♥ **www.antiracismnet.org**—A site that provides news and information about social justice and anti-racism activities.

Positive Identity

♥ **www.pointsoflight.org**—Read about more than a thousand "Daily Points of Light"—real people who have made contributions to society in large and small ways.

Asset-Building Ideas for Choosing and
Talking about Movies and TV Shows

We live in a media-saturated society. We spend huge amounts of money creating, advertising, and seeing movies and TV shows. They influence and reflect fashion, music, cultural and social trends, and sales of toys and other merchandise. Advances in technology have ensured that favorites can be watched over and over again, thus magnifying their impact.

With all of the choices and messages about which movies and TV shows are worth seeing (advertisements, reviews, awards shows, word of mouth), it can be hard to decide what to see and what to avoid. These choices are even more difficult to make regarding what is appropriate for children and young people.

Below are some ideas for how to select movies and TV shows with asset-building themes. In addition, there are suggestions for how to learn from movies and TV shows, use them to spark discussions about assets, and critique them in ways that focus on asset-building themes and messages.

Choosing Movies

♥ Find a good book or Web site that reviews movies with young people in mind. Some parenting Web sites include movie reviews. (One such Web site is www.mediafamily .org.) There are also printed guides available with information about nonviolent, nonracist, nonsexist movies and videos. Check with your local librarian for help in locating these resources.

♥ Do not go to movies when they are first released. Wait and get opinions from others before deciding what to see.

♥ Ask for suggestions of what to rent at your local video store. Tell them the kinds of things you like and do not like. They may have seen a lot of videos themselves or heard reviews from other renters. Be sure to ask about violence and vulgarity, which often go unnoticed because they are so common in movies and videos.

♥ Choose movies for children that are developmentally appropriate. For example, toddlers have relatively short attention spans and may only watch for a few minutes; an ideal length for preschoolers and elementary-age children is about 30 minutes.

♥ Preview all movies before allowing young people to watch them. If you censor a movie, be sure to explain your reasons.

Choosing TV Shows

♥ Know the rating of the TV show before you watch it. The television industry has created a TV rating system similar to the ratings for movies. For a list of the ratings and their definitions, go to www.tvguidelines.org /ratings.asp.

♥ See what the Parents Television Council says about a specific TV show. Visit www.parentstv.org. Find the show you're interested in under "Look Up a TV Show Rating." Each show has detailed information that will help you decide whether or not it's worth watching.

♥ Talk with others about their favorite TV shows and what they like about them.

♥ Encourage individuals to be intentional about their TV viewing. Rather than "grazing" for hours (turning on the television and clicking the remote control to find out what's on), check the listings first to choose specific shows you'd like to watch. Record them if you're not home when they come on.

♥ Choose TV shows that have asset-building themes. Watch TV shows that develop well-rounded characters, have interesting plots, and show characters wrestling with values and ethics.

Talking about Movies and TV Shows

♥ When watching TV or movies on DVD, make it a special family time by snuggling, having snacks, laughing together, and talking about the show afterward.

♥ Use the following questions to help you reflect on a movie or TV show you have seen, or start a conversation about a movie or TV show with family or friends:*

1. Who were the role models in the show? Who were the "villains"? Did those roles reflect stereotypes or generalizations about what certain races, cultures, or other groups are like? Were females and males equally represented?

2. Which scene best showed people building assets for other people? Which scene showed the least amount of asset building?

3. Which characters seemed to have the most assets? Which had the least? What difference did that make in the things they did and the choices they made?

4. Which values did different characters have? How did those values impact their actions?

5. Which characters seemed most empowered and in control of their lives? What helped them be that way?

6. Which character would you most like to be? Why? Which character would you least like to be? Why?

7. What are the messages about sex, alcohol and other drugs, conflict resolution, money, gender, race, class, and other issues?

8. Who were the characters who would support you the most if they were real people? Why? Who were the people you think would support you the least? Why?

9. What would you change about the show to give it a strong message about asset building?

* Note: These questions may need to be adapted depending on the type of movie and the maturity of the people having the discussion.

Spanish Handouts
Handouts 79-89

¿Qué son los Elementos
Fundamentales del Desarrollo?

¿Se ha preguntado alguna vez por qué algunos niños parecen crecer sin tropiezos mientras que otros lo hacen con tanta dificultad? ¿Le sorprende que algunos niños prosperen a pesar de circunstancias difíciles?

El Instituto Search es una organización de investigaciones, sin fines lucrativos, ubicada en Minneapolis, Minnesota, que ha estado haciendo estas mismas preguntas desde 1958. A través de estudios de cientos de miles de jóvenes por todo el país, el Instituto Search ha encontrado 40 bases esenciales para que los jóvenes tengan éxito. A estas 40 bases las llamaron Elementos Fundamentales del Desarrollo. Estos elementos fundamentales no tienen que ver con finanzas. Al contrario, son oportunidades, habilidades, relaciones, valores y autopercepciones que todos los jóvenes necesitan en sus vidas.

Estos elementos fundamentales son, al mismo tiempo, externos (cosas que otra gente proporciona a la juventud) e internos (cosas que se desarrollan dentro de sí mismos por ellos mismos). Existen cuatro categorías de elementos fundamentales externos y cuatro categorías de elementos fundamentales internos.

Elementos Fundamentales Externos

Apoyo

La gente joven necesita que su familia y muchos otros le den apoyo, se interesen por ella y le den amor. También necesita organizaciones e instituciones, como lo son las escuelas y las congregaciones que proporcionan un ambiente positivo y de apoyo. Hay seis elementos fundamentales en la categoría de apoyo:

Elemento fundamental 1— Apoyo familiar

Elemento fundamental 2— Comunicación familiar positiva

Elemento fundamental 3— Otras relaciones con adultos

Elemento fundamental 4— Una comunidad comprometida

Elemento fundamental 5— Un plantel educativo que se interesa por el (la) joven

Elemento fundamental 6— La participación de los padres en las actividades escolares

Fortalecimiento

La gente joven necesita sentirse valorada por su comunidad y tener maneras importantes para contribuir. También necesita sentirse segura. Hay cuatro elementos fundamentales en la categoría de fortalecimiento:

Elemento fundamental 7— La comunidad valora a la juventud

Elemento fundamental 8— La juventud como un recurso

Elemento fundamental 9— Servicio a los demás

Elemento fundamental 10— Seguridad

Límites y Expectativas

La gente joven necesita saber qué se espera de ella y si sus actividades y comportamientos son aceptables o inaceptables. Hay seis elementos fundamentales en la categoría de límites y expectativas:

Elemento fundamental 11— Límites familiares

Elemento fundamental 12— Límites escolares

Elemento fundamental 13— Límites vecinales

Elemento fundamental 14— El comportamiento de los adultos como ejemplo

Elemento fundamental 15— Compañeros como influencia positiva

Elemento fundamental 16— Altas expectativas

Uso Constructivo del Tiempo

La gente joven necesita pasar su tiempo de una manera positiva y saludable. Eso incluye realizar actividades en programas juveniles, en instituciones religiosas y en el hogar. Hay cuatro elementos fundamentales en la categoría de uso constructivo del tiempo:

Elemento fundamental 17— Actividades creativas

Elemento fundamental 18— Programas juveniles

Elemento fundamental 19— Comunidad religiosa

Elemento fundamental 20— Tiempo en casa

Elementos Fundamentales Internos

Compromiso Hacia el Aprendizaje

La gente joven logra lo mejor cuando desarrolla un fuerte interés por la educación y el compromiso hacia el aprendizaje. Hay cinco elementos fundamentales en la categoría de compromiso hacia el aprendizaje:

Elemento fundamental 21— Motivación por sus logros

Elemento fundamental 22— Compromiso con la escuela

Elemento fundamental 23— Tarea

Elemento fundamental 24— Preocuparse por la escuela

Elemento fundamental 25— Leer por placer

Valores Positivos

La gente joven prospera cuando desarrolla valores sólidos que guían sus decisiones. Hay seis elementos fundamentales en la categoría de valores positivos:

Elemento fundamental 26— Preocuparse por los demás

Elemento fundamental 27— Igualdad y justicia social

Elemento fundamental 28— Integridad

Elemento fundamental 29— Honestidad

Elemento fundamental 30— Responsabilidad

Elemento fundamental 31— Abstinencia

Pass It On!
Folleto 79

Capacidad Social

La gente joven se beneficia al tener habilidades y capacidades que les dan las herramientas para tomar decisiones positivas, para formar relaciones positivas y para lidiar con situaciones difíciles. Cinco elementos fundamentales forman la categoría de capacidad social:

Elemento fundamental 32— Planeación y toma de decisiones

Elemento fundamental 33— Capacidad interpersonal

Elemento fundamental 34— Capacidad cultural

Elemento fundamental 35— Habilidad de resistencia

Elemento fundamental 46— Solución pacífica de conflictos

Identidad Positiva

La gente joven necesita desarrollar un fuerte sentido de su propio poder, propósito, valor y promesa. Hay cuatro elementos fundamentales en la categoría de identidad positiva:

Elemento fundamental 37— Poder personal

Elemento fundamental 38— Autoestima

Elemento fundamental 39— Sentido de propósito

Elemento fundamental 40— Visión positiva del futuro personal

Principios para construir
elementos fundamentales

La gente joven en la encuesta del Instituto Search solamente experimenta un promedio de 19 de los 40 elementos fundamentales. Por lo tanto un compromiso para formar los elementos fundamentales debería ser una máxima prioridad para cada individuo, cada organización y cada comunidad. El Instituto Search ha identificado seis principios que pueden ayudar a formar nuestros esfuerzos para construir elementos fundamentales.

☞ Todos los niños y jóvenes necesitan los elementos fundamentales.

Las investigaciones demuestran que los jóvenes sin importar su género, edad, tipo de familia, raza o grupo étnico pueden beneficiarse por tener más elementos fundamentales. Mientras debemos continuar a prestar atención especial a los niños y jóvenes que estén en crisis o aquéllos que estén en riesgo, nuestro desafío principal es generar un tipo de atención que ayude a *todos* los jóvenes.

☞ Buenas relaciones son la clave.

Construir elementos fundamentales requiere la atención de cada persona para formar relaciones positivas y afectivas, ambas formales e informales, con los jóvenes.

☞ Todos pueden construir elementos fundamentales.

En una comunidad que forma elementos fundamentales, todos trabajan para desarrollar relaciones afectivas con los jóvenes.

☞ El construir los elementos fundamentales es un proceso continuo.

La formación de los elementos fundamentales empieza antes del nacimiento o la adopción, dándoles las herramientas a estos futuros padres para que tengan el conocimiento y las habilidades para cuidar a un bebé o a un niño(a). Y la formación de los elementos fundamentales continúa a través de la infancia, adolescencia y la edad adulta. Los jóvenes necesitan que los elementos fundamentales sean alimentados todos los días, durante todos los años de su infancia y adolescencia.

Pass It On!
Folleto 80

☛ El construir elementos fundamentales requiere de mensajes consistentes.

Para que la formación de los elementos fundamentales sea tejida en la tela de la vida de la comunidad, debe ser reforzada en todos lugares. Eso quiere decir en los hogares, escuelas, congregaciones, lugares de trabajo, clubs. Donde quiera.

☛ La duplicación y la repetición son buenas e importantes.

La gente joven necesita de tantas experiencias que construyen elementos fundamentales como sea posible.

40 Elementos Fundamentales del
Desarrollo para niños pre-escolares (edades de 3 a 5)

El Instituto Search ha identificado las siguientes bases esenciales para el desarrollo que ayudan a los niños pre-escolares de edades 3 a 5 años a crecer sanos, interesados en el bienestar común y a ser responsables.

CATEGORÍA	NOMBRE Y DEFINICIÓN DEL ELEMENTO FUNDAMENTAL
Apoyo	1. **Apoyo familiar**—Padres y/o proveedores primordiales de cuidado de niños(as) proporcionan al niño(a) con niveles altos de amor consistente y predecible, cuidado físico y atención positiva en maneras que responden a la individualidad del niño(a).
	2. **La comunicación familiar positiva**—Los padres y/o proveedores primordiales de cuidado de niños(as) se expresan de una manera positiva y respetuosa, atrayendo a niños(as) pequeños a tomar parte en conversaciones que invitan su punto de vista.
	3. **Otras relaciones con adultos**—Con el apoyo de la familia, el niño(a) experimenta relaciones cariñosas y consistentes con otros adultos fuera de la familia.
	4. **Vecinos que se preocupan**—La red de relaciones del niño(a) incluye a vecinos quienes proporcionan apoyo emocional y un sentido de pertenecer.
	5. **Un ambiente afectuoso en lugares educativos o que proporcionan cuidado de niños(as)**— Los proveedores de cuidado de niños(as) y los maestros crean un ambiente afectuoso, de aceptación, estimulación y seguro.
	6. **La participación de los padres en la educación y en el cuidado del niño(a)**—Los padres, los proveedores de cuidado de niños(as) y los maestros juntos crean un método consistente y de apoyo que fomenta el crecimiento exitoso del niño(a).
Fortale-cimiento	7. **La comunidad estima y valora a los niños(as)**—Los niños(as) son bienvenidos y se les incluye completamente en la vida comunitaria.
	8. **Los niños(as) como un recurso**—La comunidad demuestra que los niños(as) son recursos valiosos por medio de inversiones en un sistema de crianza de niños(as) de apoyo familiar y actividades de alta calidad y recursos que satisfacen las necesidades físicas, sociales y emocionales de los niños(as).
	9. **Servicio a los demás**—El niño(a) tiene la oportunidad de realizar acciones sencillas pero significativas y de interés por los demás.
	10. **Seguridad**—Los padres de los niños(as), los proveedores de cuidado de niños(as), los maestros, los vecinos y la comunidad toman acción para asegurar la salud y la seguridad de los niños(as).
Límites y Expectativas	11. **Límites familiares**—La familia proporciona supervisión consistente para el niño(a) y mantiene guías razonables por un comportamiento que el niño(a) puede comprender y lograr.
	12. **Límites en lugares educativos y que proporcionan cuidado de niños(as)**—Proveedores de cuidado de niños(as) y los educadores usan métodos positivos de disciplina y consecuencias naturales para animar la autorregulación y comportamientos aceptables.
	13. **Límites vecinales**—Los vecinos animan al niño(a) en comportamientos positivos y aceptables como también intervienen en el comportamiento negativo, de una manera de apoyo y no amenazadora.
	14. **Los adultos como ejemplo**—Los padres, los proveedores de cuidado de niños(as) y otros adultos modelan el auto control, habilidades sociales, el compromiso hacia el aprendizaje, y estilos de vida saludables.
	15. **Relaciones positivas con compañeros**—Los padres y los proveedores de cuidado de niños(as) buscan proporcionar oportunidades para que el niño(a) interactúe positivamente con otros niños(as).
	16. **Expectativas positivas**—Los padres, los proveedores de cuidado de niños(as) y los maestros animan y apoyan al niño(a) en comportarse apropiadamente, a que tome trabajos que le ofrezcan retos, y en realizar actividades a lo mejor de sus habilidades.
Uso Constructivo del Tiempo	17. **Juegos y actividades creativas**—El niño(a) tiene oportunidades diariamente para jugar en maneras que le permiten la expresión propia, actividad física, e interacción con otros.
	18. **Programas fuera del hogar y comunitarios**—El niño(a) experimenta programas en lugares bien mantenidos y que son bien diseñados y guiados por adultos competentes y cariñosos.
	19. **La comunidad religiosa**—El niño(a) participa en actividades religiosas apropiadas a su edad y en relaciones afectuosas que cultivan su desarrollo espiritual.
	20. **Tiempo en casa**—El niño(a) pasa la mayor parte de su tiempo en casa participando en actividades familiares y jugando constructivamente, con los padres guiando el uso de la televisión y los juegos electrónicos.

ELEMENTOS FUNDAMENTALES EXTERNOS

Pass It On!

Folleto 81

CATEGORÍA	NOMBRE Y DEFINICIÓN DEL ELEMENTO FUNDAMENTAL
Compromiso Hacia el Aprendizaje	**21. Motivación por la superación**—El niño(a) responde a experiencias nuevas con curiosidad y energía, resultando en el placer de lograr nuevo aprendizaje y habilidades. **22. Compromisos a experiencias del aprendizaje**—El niño(a) participa completamente en una variedad de actividades que ofrecen oportunidades de aprendizaje. **23. Conexión entre el hogar y programas**—El niño(a) experimenta seguridad, consistencia y conexiones entre el hogar y programas fuera del hogar y actividades de aprendizaje. **24. Acercamiento a los programas**—El niño(a) forma conexiones significativas con el cuidado fuera del hogar y programas educativos. **25. Lectura temprana**—El niño(a) disfruta una variedad de actividades de pre-lectura, incluyendo adultos quienes le leen diariamente, ver y manipular los libros, jugar con una variedad de medios, y demuestra interés en dibujos, letras y números.
Valores Positivos	**26. Preocuparse por los demás**—El niño(a) empieza a demostrar empatía, comprensión, y está al tanto de los sentimientos de los demás. **27. Igualdad y la justicia social**—El niño(a) empieza a demostrar preocupación por las personas a quienes se les excluye de juegos y otras actividades o a quienes no se les trata justamente porque son diferentes. **28. Integridad**—El niño(a) empieza a expresar su punto de vista apropiadamente y a luchar por lo que él o ella siente que es lo justo y correcto. **29. Honestidad**—El niño(a) empieza a comprender la diferencia entre la verdad y la mentira, dice la verdad según su alcance de comprensión. **30. Responsabilidad**—El niño empieza a cumplir con trabajos simples para cuidarse a sí mismo(a) o para cuidar a otros. **31. Autorregulación**—El niño incrementadamente puede identificar, regular y controlar su comportamiento en maneras saludables, usando el apoyo de adultos constructivamente particularmente en situaciones estresantes.
Capacidad Social	**32. Planificación y toma de decisiones**—El niño(a) empieza a planear para su futuro inmediato, escogiendo de varias opciones y tratando de resolver problemas. **33. Habilidades interpersonales**—El niño(a) coopera, comparte, juega con armonía y conforta a los que están angustiados. **34. Conocimiento y sensibilidad cultural**—El niño empieza a aprender sobre su propia identidad cultural y demuestra aceptación hacia personas que son física, racial, étnica y culturalmente diferentes a él o ella. **35. Habilidad de resistencia**—El niño(a) empieza a sentir peligro con exactitud, a buscar ayuda en adultos de confianza, y a resistir presión de sus compañeros a participar en comportamientos inaceptables o de riesgo. **36. Solución pacífica de conflictos**—El niño(a) empieza a comprometerse y a resolver conflictos sin utilizar agresión física o vocabulario que hiere.
Identidad Positiva	**37. Poder personal**—El niño(a) puede hacer decisiones que dan un sentido de tener algo de influencia sobre las cosas que pasan en su vida. **38. Autoestima**—El niño(a) se quiere a sí mismo y tiene una percepción creciente de ser valorado por otros. **39. Sentido de propósito**—El niño(a) anticipa nuevas oportunidades, experiencias y logros en su crecimiento. **40. Visión positiva del futuro personal**—El niño(a) encuentra el mundo interesante y divertido y siente que él o ella tiene un lugar positivo en él.

ELEMENTOS FUNDAMENTALES INTERNOS

40 Elementos Fundamentales del
Desarrollo para la pre-adolescencia (edades de 8 a 12)

El Instituto Search ha identificado las siguientes bases esenciales para el desarrollo que ayudan a niños(as) de edades 8 a 12 años a crecer sanos, interesados en el bienestar común y a ser responsables.

CATEGORÍA	NOMBRE Y DEFINICIÓN DEL ELEMENTO FUNDAMENTAL
Apoyo	1. **Apoyo familiar**—La vida familiar brinda altos niveles de amor y apoyo.
	2. **La comunicación familiar positiva**—El padre y el niño(a) se comunican en una manera positiva. El niño(a) se siente cómodo(a) en buscar consejo y consuelo en sus padres.
	3. **Otras relaciones con adultos**—El niño(a) recibe el apoyo de otros adultos además de sus padres.
	4. **Una comunidad comprometida**—El niño(a) percibe el interés de sus vecinos por su bienestar.
	5. **Un plantel educativo que se interesa por los niños(as)**—Las relaciones positivas con los maestros y los compañeros proporcionan un ambiente escolar que se interesa por los niños(as) y los ánima.
	6. **La participación de los padres en la escuela**—Los padres participan activamente ayudando a los niños(as) a tener éxito en la escuela.
Fortalecimiento	7. **La comunidad valora a los niños**—El niño(a) se siente valorado(a) y apreciado(a) por los adultos en la comunidad.
	8. **Los niños(as) como un recurso**—El niño(a) es incluido(a) en las decisiones en el hogar y en la comunidad.
	9. **Servicio a los demás**—El niño(a) tiene la oportunidad de ayudar a otros en la comunidad.
	10. **Seguridad**—El niño(a) se siente seguro(a) en casa, en la escuela y en el vecindario.
Límites y Expectativas	11. **Límites familiares**—La familia tiene reglas y consecuencias claras y consistentes y vigila el paradero del niño(a).
	12. **Límites escolares**—La escuela proporciona reglas y consecuencias claras.
	13. **Límites vecinales**—Los vecinos asumen la responsabilidad de vigilar el comportamiento del niño(a).
	14. **Los adultos como ejemplo**—Los padres y otros adultos en la familia del niño(a), tal como otros adultos fuera de la familia dan un ejemplo de comportamiento positivo y responsable.
	15. **Influencia positiva de los compañeros**—Los amigos más cercanos del niño(a) dan un ejemplo de comportamiento positivo y responsable.
	16. **Altas expectativas**—Los padres y los maestros esperan que el niño(a) haga su mejor esfuerzo en la escuela y en otras actividades.
Uso Constructivo del Tiempo	17. **Actividades creativas**—El niño(a) participa en música, arte, drama o escritura creativa dos o más veces a la semana.
	18. **Programas para niños(as)**—El niño(a) participa dos o más veces a la semana en actividades escolares extracurriculares o en programas estructurados para niños(as) en la comunidad.
	19. **Comunidad religiosa**—El niño(a) asiste a programas o servicios religiosos una o más veces a la semana.
	20. **Tiempo en casa**—La mayoría de los días el niño(a) pasa algún tiempo en ambas interacciones de alta calidad con sus padres y en hacer cosas en casa además de ver la televisión o juegos de video.

ELEMENTOS FUNDAMENTALES EXTERNOS

Pass It On!

CATEGORÍA	NOMBRE Y DEFINICIÓN DEL ELEMENTO FUNDAMENTAL

ELEMENTOS FUNDAMENTALES INTERNOS

Compromiso Hacia el Aprendizaje

21. **Motivación por sus logros**—El niño(a) está motivado(a) y se esfuerza para sobresalir en la escuela.

22. **Compromiso hacia el aprendizaje**—El niño(a) responde al aprendizaje, es atento y está activamente comprometido(a) a aprender en la escuela y disfruta participar en actividades de aprendizaje fuera de la escuela.

23. **Tarea**—Regularmente el niño(a) entrega su tarea a tiempo.

24. **Acercamiento con adultos en la escuela**—El niño(a) se preocupa por los maestros y otros adultos en la escuela.

25. **Leer por placer**—El niño(a) disfruta de la lectura y lee para divertirse la mayoría de los días durante la semana.

Valores Positivos

26. **Preocuparse por los demás**—Los padres le dicen al niño(a) que es importante ayudar a otras personas.

27. **Igualdad y la justicia social**—Los padres le dicen al niño(a) que es importante defender la igualdad de derechos para todas las personas.

28. **Integridad**—Los padres le dicen al niño(a) que es importante defender las creencias propias.

29. **Honestidad**—Los padres le dicen al niño(a) que es importante decir la verdad.

30. **Responsabilidad**—Los padres le dicen al niño(a) que es importante aceptar responsabilidad por su propio comportamiento.

31. **Estilo de vida saludable**—Los padres le dicen al niño(a) que es importante tener buenos hábitos de salud y un entendimiento saludable de la sexualidad.

Capacidad Social

32. **Planificación y toma de decisiones**—El niño(a) piensa acerca de las decisiones y regularmente está contento(a) con los resultados de sus decisiones.

33. **Capacidad interpersonal**—El niño(a) se preocupa por los demás y le afectan los sentimientos de otras personas, disfruta de hacer amigos y cuando está frustrado(a) o enojado(a), trata de calmarse a sí mismo(a).

34. **Capacidad cultural**—El niño(a) conoce y se siente cómodo(a) con gente de diferente marco cultural, racial, étnico y con su propia identidad cultural.

35. **Habilidad de resistencia**—El niño(a) puede mantenerse alejado(a) de personas que pudieran meterlo(a) en problemas y es capaz de negarse a hacer cosas incorrectas y peligrosas.

36. **Solución pacífica de conflictos**—El niño(a) trata de resolver conflictos sin violencia.

Identidad Positiva

37. **Poder personal**—El niño(a) siente que tiene algo de influencia sobre las cosas que suceden en su vida.

38. **Autoestima**—Al niño(a) le gusta ser y se siente orgulloso de la persona que es.

39. **Sentido de propósito**—El niño(a) piensa algunas veces sobre el significado de la vida y si hay un propósito para su vida.

40. **Visión positiva del futuro**—El niño(a) es optimista sobre su futuro personal.

40 Elementos Fundamentales del
Desarrollo para los adolescentes (edades de 12 a 18)

El Instituto Search ha identificado las siguientes bases esenciales para el desarrollo que ayudan a los jóvenes a crecer sanos, interesados en el bienestar común y a ser responsables.

CATEGORÍA	NOMBRE Y DEFINICIÓN DEL ELEMENTO FUNDAMENTAL
Apoyo	1. **Apoyo familiar**—La vida familiar brinda altos niveles de amor y apoyo.
	2. **Comunicación familiar positiva**—El (La) joven y sus padres se comunican positivamente. Los jóvenes están dispuestos a buscar consejo y consuelo en sus padres.
	3. **Otras relaciones con adultos**—Además de sus padres, los jóvenes reciben apoyo de tres o más personas adultas que no son sus padres.
	4. **Una comunidad comprometida**—El (La) joven experimenta el interés de sus vecinos por su bienestar.
	5. **Un plantel educativo que se interesa por el (la) joven**—La escuela proporciona un ambiente que anima y se preocupa por la juventud.
	6. **La participación de los padres en las actividades escolares**—Los padres participan activamente ayudando a los jóvenes a tener éxito en la escuela.
Fortalecimiento	7. **La comunidad valora a la juventud**—El (La) joven percibe que los adultos en la comunidad valoran a la juventud.
	8. **La juventud como un recurso**—Se le brinda a los jóvenes la oportunidad de tomar un papel útil en la comunidad.
	9. **Servicio a los demás**—La gente joven participa brindando servicios a su comunidad una hora o más a la semana.
	10. **Seguridad**—Los jóvenes se sienten seguros en casa, en la escuela y en el vecindario.
Límites y Expectativas	11. **Límites familiares**—La familia tiene reglas y consecuencias bien claras, además vigila las actividades de los jóvenes.
	12. **Límites escolares**—En la escuela proporcionan reglas y consecuencias bien claras.
	13. **Límites vecinales**—Los vecinos asumen la responsabilidad de vigilar el comportamiento de los jóvenes.
	14. **El comportamiento de los adultos como ejemplo**—Los padres y otros adultos tienen un comportamiento positivo y responsable.
	15. **Compañeros como influencia positiva**—Los mejores amigos del (la) joven son un buen ejemplo de comportamiento responsable.
	16. **Altas expectativas**—Ambos padres y maestros motivan a los jóvenes para que tengan éxito.
Uso Constructivo del Tiempo	17. **Actividades creativas**—Los jóvenes pasan tres horas o más a la semana en lecciones de música, teatro u otras artes.
	18. **Programas juveniles**—Los jóvenes pasan tres horas o más a la semana practicando algún deporte, o en organizaciones en la escuela o de la comunidad.
	19. **Comunidad religiosa**—Los jóvenes pasan una hora o más a la semana en actividades organizadas por alguna institución religiosa.
	20. **Tiempo en casa**—Los jóvenes conviven con sus amigos "sin un propósito en particular" dos noches o menos por semana.

ELEMENTOS FUNDAMENTALES EXTERNOS

Pass It On!
Folleto 83

ELEMENTOS FUNDAMENTALES INTERNOS	CATEGORÍA	NOMBRE Y DEFINICIÓN DEL ELEMENTO FUNDAMENTAL
	Compromiso Hacia el Aprendizaje	**21. Motivación por sus logros**—El (La) joven es motivado(a) para que salga bien en la escuela.
		22. Compromiso hacia la escuela—El (La) joven participa activamente en el aprendizaje.
		23. Tarea—El (La) joven afirma hacer tarea escolar por lo menos durante una hora cada día de clases.
		24. Preocuparse por la escuela—Al (A la) joven le importa su escuela.
		25. Leer por placer—El (La) joven lee por placer tres horas o más por semana.
	Valores Positivos	**26. Preocuparse por los demás**—El (La) joven valora ayudar a los demás.
		27. Igualdad y justicia social—Para el (la) joven tiene mucho valor el promover la igualdad y el reducir el hambre y la pobreza.
		28. Integridad—El (La) joven actúa con convicción y defiende sus creencias.
		29. Honestidad—El (La) joven "dice la verdad aún cuando esto no sea fácil".
		30. Responsabilidad—El (La) joven acepta y toma responsabilidad por su persona.
		31. Abstinencia—El (La) joven cree que es importante no estar activo(a) sexualmente, ni usar alcohol u otras drogas.
	Capacidad Social	**32. Planeación y toma de decisiones**—El (La) joven sabe cómo planear y hacer elecciones.
		33. Capacidad interpersonal—El (La) joven tiene empatía, es sensible y hábil para hacer amistades.
		34. Capacidad cultural—El (La) joven tiene conocimiento de y sabe convivir con gente de diferente marco cultural, racial o étnico.
		35. Habilidad de resistencia—El (La) joven puede resistir la presión negativa de los compañeros así como las situaciones peligrosas.
		36. Solución pacífica de conflictos—El (La) joven busca resolver los conflictos sin violencia.
	Identidad Positiva	**37. Poder personal**—El (La) joven siente que él o ella tiene el control de "las cosas que le suceden".
		38. Autoestima—El (La) joven afirma tener una alta autoestima.
		39. Sentido de propósito—El (La) joven afirma que "mi vida tiene un propósito".
		40. Visión positiva del futuro personal—El (La) joven es optimista sobre su futuro mismo.

Ideas para que los padres y guardianes formen elementos fundamentales

Ser un padre o un guardián puede ser un trabajo muy difícil—no es sorprendente, ¿verdad? La mayoría de padres y guardianes tienen cosas que aman sobre su papel de ser padre, así como también tienen problemas con sus hijos(as) con los cuales tienen que lidiar. Sin embargo, lo que puede ser sorprendente es que una de las mejores maneras para lidiar con los problemas es enfocarse en lo positivo. Las investigaciones demuestran que una manera más efectiva para criar hijos(as) sanos y competentes es concentrarse en construir los Elementos Fundamentales del Desarrollo. Estos elementos fundamentales forman la base que la gente joven necesita para tomar decisiones sanas y para tener éxito en la vida. En cuanto más elementos fundamentales tengan sus hijos(as), más fuerte será esta fundación.

Probablemente hay muchas cosas que usted ya hace por sus hijos que construyen elementos fundamentales—aunque usted no les llame así. Aquí hay varias maneras que usted puede usar para construir elementos fundamentales intencionalmente:

➤ **Pongo la lista de los Elementos Fundamentales del Desarrollo en la puerta de su refrigerador. Diariamente haga por lo menos una cosa para cada miembro de la familia que construya elementos fundamentales.**

➤ Haga una conexión con otros padres que estén interesados en construir elementos fundamentales. Forme relaciones positivas en su vecindario, en el trabajo, por medio de una congregación o una organización de educación para padres.

➤ **Regularmente haga cosas con sus hijos(as), incluyendo proyectos alrededor de la casa, actividades recreativas y proyectos de servicio. Tomen turnos planeando actividades que pueden hacer juntos como familia.**

➤ Como familia, coman al menos una comida juntos cada día.

➤ **Negocie las reglas familiares y las consecuencias por romperlas.**

➤ Desarrolle una declaración familiar con la misión de enfocarse en construir elementos fundamentales. Y luego, úsela para tomar decisiones y fijar prioridades.

➤ **Hable sobre sus valores y sus prioridades, y viva de tal manera que sea consistente con ellos.**

➤ Dé a sus hijos(as) mucho apoyo y aprobación mientras que también los reta a tomar responsabilidades y lograr independencia.

➤ **Si está solo como padre o madre, busque a otros adultos de ambos géneros que sean un ejemplo positivo, mentores o guías para sus hijos(as).**

➤ Cultive sus propios elementos fundamentales pasando tiempo con gente que se interesa por usted y que le apoya. También aproveche las oportunidades para aprender cosas nuevas, contribuya a su comunidad y diviértase. Cuidará mejor a sus hijos(as) si se cuida a usted mismo(a).

➤ **Piense en la manera que lo criaron y cómo eso afecta su relación con sus hijos(as). Si hay partes de su relación con sus padres que fueron muy difíciles o que interfieren en su manera de criar a sus hijos(as), considere hablarle a alguien acerca de sus asuntos.**

➤ No deje que nadie en su familia (incluyéndose a usted) vea demasiada televisión. Busque otras actividades interesantes y significativas que sus hijos(as) puedan hacer—algunas con usted, algunas con sus amigos y otras por sí mismos.

➤ **Aprenda lo más que pueda sobre las necesidades de sus hijos(as) en su edad actual.**

➤ Reconozca que sus hijos(as) necesitan más que solo el apoyo financiero. Ellos también necesitan apoyo emocional e intelectual. Cree un balance de tiempo familiar con otras prioridades tales como trabajo, recreación y pasatiempos.

➤ **No espere a que surjan problemas antes de hablar con los maestros de sus hijos. Mantenga un contacto regular con ellos acerca del rendimiento de sus hijos(as) en la escuela y sobre lo que usted puede hacer para ayudarles a aprender.**

➤ Piense en los adolescentes como si fueran adultos en entrenamiento. Enséñeles cosas prácticas tales como cambiar una llanta a un automóvil, preparar una comida o crear un presupuesto mensual.

➤ **Entérese sobre las diferencias de cómo usted se relaciona con sus hijos(as). ¿Se siente más cómodo con un género que con el otro? Si es así, ¿por qué? ¿Qué impacto tiene eso en su familia?**

➤ Hable con sus hijos(as) sobre los 40 Elementos Fundamentales del Desarrollo. Pídales sugerencias para fortalecer sus propios elementos fundamentales.

➤ **Haga actividades que involucran a más de una generación con otros familiares y con otros adultos y familias del vecindario.**

➤ Sea un forjador de elementos fundamentales para otra gente joven en su vida.

➤ **Recuerde que no está solo. Otras personas que construyen elementos fundamentales en las vidas de sus hijos(as) incluyen entrenadores, proveedores de cuidado de niños, maestros de educación de la fe, líderes de clubs y vecinos. Trabaje con estas personas para dar mensajes consistentes a sus hijos(as) sobre límites y valores.**

➤ Conozca a los amigos de sus hijos(as)-y a los padres de los amigos. Hable con ellos sobre los Elementos Fundamentales del Desarrollo.

Ideas para que la gente joven forme elementos fundamentales

Tú puedes hacer una diferencia para tí mismo y para tus compañeros aprendiendo sobre y construyendo los elementos fundamentales. Algunos adolescentes han empezado por aprender los nombres de la mayoría de sus compañeros en la escuela. Algunos construyen los elementos fundamentales a través de formar amistades con niños menores. Otros han enfocado sus esfuerzos en hacer una diferencia en su congregación o comunidad. Aquí hay ideas de cómo empezar a ser un forjador de elementos fundamentales:

➤ Apréndete los nombres de tus vecinos (incluyendo adultos, niños y otros adolescentes). Pídele a uno de tus padres que te presente con los vecinos que no conozcas.

➤ **Pon los 40 Elementos Fundamentales del Desarrollo en tu habitación o en tu armario. Escoge uno de los elementos fundamentales cada día y enfócate en fomentar éste en tus amigos.**

➤ Vive una variedad de experiencias y actividades en música, teatro, arte y atletismo, en la escuela y en tu comunidad.

➤ **Participa en por lo menos un club, grupo, equipo o deporte—o busca algo creativo que te guste tal como la actuación o la música.**

➤ Conoce a un adulto a quien admiras.

➤ **Reemplaza acciones humillantes con acciones positivas.**

➤ Escribe una nota o llama a una de las personas principales que construye los elementos fundamentales en tu vida. Agradécele por hacer una diferencia en tu vida.

➤ **Piensa en tus mejores amigos. ¿Te ayudan a levantarte el ánimo o te bajan el ánimo? ¿Cómo forman ellos los elementos fundamentales en tí? ¿Cómo formas tú los elementos fundamentales en ellos?**

➤ Anda más allá de lo habitual para saludar a tus vecinos.

➤ **Limita la cantidad de televisión que ves. Escoge los programas que realmente te gustan y no veas cualquier programa.**

➤ Se voluntario en un hogar de ancianos local, un centro comunitario o un hospital para animales.

➤ **Toma un curso para ayudar a resolver conflictos.**

➤ Empieza un club de libros con tus amigos y lee solamente por diversión.

➤ **Practica diferentes maneras de decir "no" cuando la gente trate de hacer que tú hagas cosas que realmente no quieres hacer.**

➤ Habla sobre los 40 Elementos Fundamentales del Desarrollo con tu familia. ¿Cuáles elementos fundamentales piensan los miembros de tu familia que son los más fuertes en tu familia?

➤ **Si tienes un trabajo de medio tiempo durante el año escolar, limita tu horario de trabajo para dar tiempo a tus trabajos escolares, hacer cosas con la familia y amigos y otras actividades.**

➤ Identifica las aptitudes de cada miembro de tu familia y aprende de ellos. Si tu hermana es buenísima en geografía, búscala cuando estés leyendo un mapa o necesites ayuda con una tarea de geografía. Si tu papá es un genio en matemáticas, búscalo para hacer un plan de ahorros o para ayuda con problemas de matemáticas.

➤ **Discute con la gente joven en tu vecindario sobre lo que es bueno de vivir donde vives. También discute las maneras en las que puedes ayudar a mejorar tu vecindario.**

➤ Aunque tu familia te proporcione un lugar caluroso, cariñoso, y de apoyo en el cual crecer, también busca apoyo por medio de adultos en tu escuela, en organizaciones comunitarias o en una comunidad de fe. En cuanto más relaciones positivas con adultos tengas, será mejor.

➤ **Examina las actividades que tienes fuera de la escuela. ¿Sientes que tienes desafíos? ¿Disfrutas de las actividades? ¿Sientes que tienes tiempo para las actividades, para terminar tus tareas y también tienes tiempo para tí mismo, tu familia y tus amigos? Si no es así, considera hacer algunos cambios.**

➤ Busca adultos mentores y a personas que son ejemplos sanos a seguir.

➤ **Involúcrate en un asunto social que te interesa tal como la pobreza, los dere-**chos civiles, especies a punto de extinción, el hambre, el abuso y la negligencia de niños, el medio ambiente o la discriminación.

➤ Involúcrate en la comunidad por medio de ser un voluntario.

➤ **Desarrolla una relación positiva con un niño por medio de cuidarlo, jugando a la pelota con un vecino o siendo voluntario como entrenador o asistente de entrenador.**

➤ Déjales saber a tus amigos que estás disponible cuando ellos necesiten a alguien con quien hablar. Si lo necesitan, ayúdales a obtener asistencia adicional de un consejero, trabajador social, padre u otro adulto.

➤ **Busca a gente e información que te ayude a hacer que tus sueños y planes futuros se hagan realidad.**

➤ Recuerda que los niños menores te ven como un ejemplo a seguir. Toma tiempo para saludarlos y hablarles cuando los veas, especialmente en la escuela.

➤ **Cuando ves a alguien maltratando a otro trata de poner un alto si puedes hacerlo de una manera pacífica. Si es necesario, lleva el problema a un adulto.**

Ideas para vecinos y grupos vecindarios para que formen los elementos fundamentales

Un vecindario es más que sólo un lugar en donde la gente duerme y come. Un vecindario puede y debe ser una comunidad importante en la cual la gente de todas las edades se siente segura y como si alguien se preocupa por ella. Este tipo de vecindario no es la norma en la mayoría de las comunidades, pero con un enfoque en construir los elementos fundamentales lo podría ser. Dos de los 40 Elementos Fundamentales del Desarrollo (4—una comunidad comprometida; y el 13—límites vecinales) se enfocan específicamente en el papel importante que los vecinos tienen en construir elementos fundamentales. Aquí hay ideas de cómo los vecinos pueden construir éstos y otros elementos fundamentales:

Individuos

➤ **Apréndase los nombres de los jóvenes que viven a su alrededor. Entérese acerca de las cosas que les interesan.**

➤ Trate a los vecinos de cualquier edad con el mismo respeto y cortesía; espere a que ellos lo traten a usted con respeto y cortesía también.

➤ **Si vive en un departamento o condominio, pase algún tiempo en lugares donde comúnmente se reúne la gente, tal como los escalones, patios, salones de reuniones, piscinas, lavanderías y entradas principales. Salude y hable con otras personas allí. Si tiene un patio enfrente de su casa, pase tiempo allí.**

➤ Tome responsabilidad propia para construir el elemento fundamental 13: límites vecinales; cuando vea a alguien en su vecindario haciendo algo que usted piense que es inapropiado, hable con él o ella acerca de por qué eso le molesta. Cuando usted vea a alguien haciendo algo agradable-recogiendo la basura, por ejemplo-dígales cuanto usted lo agradece.

➤ **Encuentre otros vecinos que quieran hacer un compromiso de largo plazo para construir elementos fundamentales. Empiece a desarrollar estrategias para trabajar juntos en construir elementos fundamentales en su vecindario.**

➤ Tome tiempo para jugar o sólo para pasarlo con la gente joven de su cuadra o en su edificio. Anímelos a conversar y escuche lo que ellos tienen que decir.

➤ **Invite a los vecinos a su casa (especialmente a los que tienen niños o adolescentes). Conózcanse y entérense de lo que tienen en común.**

➤ De vez en cuando, deje mensajes (con tiza en la banqueta, o cuelgue una nota en la puerta) diciendo cuánto aprecia a cierto vecino. Haga esto para los vecinos de todas las edades.

➤ **Si tiene hijos(as), hable con otros padres sobre los límites y expectativas que ellos tienen para sus hijos(as). Discuta cómo ustedes pueden apoyarse el uno al otro en áreas en las que están de acuerdo.**

➤ Averigüe qué es lo que usted puede proporcionar a los jóvenes en su vecindario. ¿Puede poner un aro de baloncesto? ¿Puede ofrecer algún espacio para un jardín vecinal? ¿Puede dar una hora de su tiempo durante el fin de semana para jugar a la pelota con gente joven que vive cerca de usted?

➤ **Si tiene preocupaciones acerca de su vecindario, hable con otros vecinos sobre sus sentimientos. Si otros comparten sus preocupaciones, forme un grupo para tratar de resolverlas. Aún si usted no resuelve todos los problemas, usted fortalecerá su vecindario por medio del proceso.**

➤ Asista a un juego, una actuación o un evento en el cual esté participando un niño(a) o adolescente del vecindario. Felicítelo después del evento.

➤ **Entérese sobre las graduaciones y otros eventos de gran importancia en las vidas de los niños(as).**

➤ Una vez que conozca a sus vecinos, aprenda más sobre sus familiares y amigos. Algunas personas ancianas tienen nietos que les visitan. En otros casos los padres pueden tener custodia de sus niños(as) ciertos días de la semana. Conozca a esta gente joven que visita periódicamente.

➤ **Ponga atención cuando usted vea a un joven. Tome tiempo para sonreír y saludarlo. Si tiene unos minutos, hágale unas preguntas y exprese su interés por él o ella. Haga esto mientras camina, cuando espera el autobús o cuando espera en una fila en el supermercado.**

Grupos

➤ Empiece un grupo del vecindario. Enfóquese en la seguridad, el mejoramiento vecinal o sólo en divertirse. Involucre a la gente joven en este grupo. A menudo ellos tienen ideas y soluciones creativas.

➤ **Organice un intercambio de libros en el vecindario. Pida a los vecinos que donen libros que ya han leído e invite a todos a que vengan a encontrar libros nuevos.**

➤ Reúnase con los padres del vecindario y otros adultos que se preocupan para averiguar como los vecinos pueden ayudar a los niños(as) y adolescentes con la tarea. Considere encontrar adultos dispuestos a ser "compañeros de estudio" para ellos.

➤ **Empiece un programa vecinal para estar al tanto. Forme grupos pequeños y estén al tanto de cada uno regularmente. Si alguien necesita ayuda o apoyo, junte un grupo para ayudarlo.**

➤ Si tiene problemas de crimen o seguridad en su vecindario, hable regularmente con el departamento del policía local para averiguar lo que está pasando para resolver el problema. Pregúnteles qué pueden hacer usted y otros vecinos para hacer una diferencia.

Ideas para maestros para construir elementos fundamentales

Enseñar es tocar una vida para siempre. Los maestros tiene un potencial poderoso para construir elementos fundamentales. Además de los elementos fundamentales del compromiso hacia el aprendizaje (21–25), otros cinco elementos fundamentales (3: otras relaciones con adultos; 5: un plantel educativo que se interesa por el/la joven; 8: la juventud como un recurso; 12: límites escolares; y 14: el comportamiento de los adultos como ejemplo) se enfocan en la importancia del papel del maestro. Abajo hay algunas sugerencias acerca de lo que los maestros pueden hacer para construir elementos fundamentales. Estas sugerencias intentan dar algunas ideas para saber cómo empezar. Posiblemente necesiten ser modificadas o adaptadas dependiendo del grado que usted enseña; si usted es un maestro de salón de clase, especialista o maestro de recursos; y la naturaleza de su medio ambiente escolar.

Para construir elementos fundamentales en general

➤ **Ponga la lista de los elementos fundamentales en su salón de clase.**

➤ Dedique un tablón de anuncios en su salón de clase para poner mensajes que construyan elementos fundamentales.

➤ **Si su comunidad tiene alguna iniciativa para construir elementos fundamentales, involúcrese.**

➤ Proporcione entrenamiento para usar la estructura de los elementos fundamentales a todos los voluntarios y al personal de apoyo con quienes usted trabaja.

➤ **Planifique actividades de aprendizaje para construir elementos fundamentales como parte del currículo (por ejemplo, proyectos para brindar servicios a la comunidad, entrenamiento sobre habilidades sociales, o establezca un tiempo para leer por placer).**

➤ Ponga en su protector de pantalla en su computadora un mensaje que construye elementos fundamentales. Una escuela usó el lema "¡Envuelva con sus Brazos a los Niños de Cherry Creek . . . Construya Elementos Fundamentales!"

Apoyo

➤ **Salude a los estudiantes por su nombre cuando los vea.**

➤ Mande una carta a los padres presentándoles la idea de construir elementos fundamentales y luego úselos como puntos para comenzar discusiones en conferencias con los padres y estudiantes.

➤ **Reúnase con otros maestros y desarrollen maneras para ayudar a los estudiantes a tener éxito. Una escuela en Wisconsin, preparó lo que denominaron DATES (Developing Assets to Encourage Success – Desarrollando los Elementos Fundamentales para Animar el Éxito) reuniones que son diseñadas para ayudar a estudiantes que están batallando académicamente.**

➤ Anime el acceso de por lo menos un adulto que se preocupa por cada estudiante en el establecimiento. Los salones designados pueden facilitar esto.

> Proporcione recursos para construir elementos fundamentales a padres de familia.

Fortalecimiento

> Enseñe a los estudiantes sobre los 40 elementos fundamentales y ayúdeles a fijar metas para los elementos fundamentales que ellos quieran desarrollar (dos recursos para hacer esto son *Me@My Best* y *Take It to the Next Level*, publicado por Search Institute).

> Proporcione oportunidades para aprender por medio de servicios. Ayude a los estudiantes a planificar y tomar decisiones de cómo proporcionar servicio a otros.

> Fortalezca a los estudiantes animándolos a contar sus historias a través de autobiografías escritas y visuales.

Límites y Expectativas

> Trabaje con los estudiantes para establecer límites escolares. Ponga una serie de reglas escritas en lugares visibles: corredores, salones de clase, cafetería, gimnasio y otras áreas comunes. Haga copias de las reglas y tenga un formulario de acuerdo para que padres y estudiantes lo firmen, indicando su deseo de permanecer dentro de los límites.

> Establezca expectativas altas y claras para el comportamiento y el resultado de aprendizaje del estudiante.

> Desarrolle símbolos visuales de los ele-

Uso Constructivo del Tiempo

mentos fundamentales. Por ejemplo, murales hechos cooperativamente pueden demostrar la importancia del trabajo en conjunto para fortalecer a la comunidad. Los estudiantes de arte

pueden crear autorretratos que reflejen sus elementos fundamentales.

> Agradezca a otros maestros, miembros del personal y estudiantes cuando los encuentre construyendo elementos fundamentales.

> Demuestre sensibilidad respecto a los estudiantes que participan en actividades extracurriculares. Algunos maestros hacen una costumbre de siempre permitir al menos dos noches para que los estudiantes puedan completar sus tareas.

> Lea biografías o vea películas sobre músicos u otros artistas. Discuta los elementos fundamentales que los estudiantes ven en las vidas de esas personas.

> Discuta música, películas, otro arte y entretenimiento actuales y los mensajes que éstos envían. ¿Construyen los elementos fundamentales, o no?

> Discuta los elementos fundamentales de los personajes en historias, lecciones de

Compromiso Hacia el Aprendizaje

historia y eventos actuales. Por ejemplo, cuando estudien Romeo y Julieta, hable sobre cómo la falta de elementos fundamentales puede llevarlo a tragedias. Cambie la historia construyendo elementos fundamentales para los dos personajes principales.

> Use los elementos fundamentales como el enfoque en las tareas.

> Escoja una citación del día la cual tenga un enfoque en los elementos fundamentales y pida a los estudiantes que hablen sobre ella.

> Introduzca a los estudiantes a sitios en el Internet que tengan temas de construir elementos fundamentales.

> Lea biografías de personajes quienes han realizado sus sueños. Hable sobre

los elementos fundamentales que ayudaron a esas personas a ser exitosas.

➤ Pida a los estudiantes que reúnan información sobre sus héroes— ya sean famosos o no. Luego tenga

Valores Positivos

discusiones en grupos pequeños o como clase entera sobre qué valores parecen tener esos héroes y cómo esos valores los guían a ser quienes son y lo que hacen.

➤ **Como clase, creen una lista de valores compartidos. Vea los elementos fundamentales de valores positivos (26–31) como una referencia para empezar. Hable sobre lo que se necesita para sostener estos valores. Establezca límites y expectativas basados en esos valores.**

➤ Proporcione un proceso en el salón de clase para establecer y evaluar metas mutuas. Tal proceso fortalece a los estudiantes y activa-

Capacidad Social

mente los compromete hacia su aprendizaje.

➤ **Anime la planificación a través del uso de calendarios y agendas estudiantiles.**

➤ Utilice recursos en su comunidad que ayuden a enseñar la capacidad cultural (elemento fundamental 34). Considere que

estudiantes organicen una semana de conciencia a la diversidad, una feria cultural o alguna otra manera de aprender sobre los antecedentes y las culturas de cada uno.

➤ **No permita que los estudiantes se salgan con la suya al agredir a otros o al pelear.**

➤ Hable con ellos sobre cómo resolver conflictos pacíficamente.

➤ **Use "entrevistas de fortalecimiento" con los estudiantes para ayudarlos a identificar sus elementos fundamentales**

Identidad Positiva

y sus fuentes de apoyo.

➤ Asista a conciertos, programas y actividades en las que sus estudiantes se involucren.

➤ **Felicite los éxitos con una nota escrita, una llamada a sus casas o un elogio verbal.**

➤ Cree archivos de planificación de vida que sigan al estudiante desde el fin de un año escolar hasta el comienzo del próximo año escolar e incluya metas, sueños y esperanzas. Éstos pueden ser una herramienta importante para el estudiante—y los maestros—para mantener una historia de logros y desafíos.

Ideas para construir elementos funda-mentales para personal de apoyo estudiantil

Como consejero escolar, trabajador social, bibliotecario, enfermero u otro miembro de personal de apoyo estudiantil usted tiene contacto con muchos estudiantes cada día. Aunque usted no sea capaz de desarrollar una buena relación con cada uno de ellos, hay cosas que son únicas sobre su papel que lo convierte en un forjador clave de elementos fundamentales en su escuela. Usted puede conectar estudiantes con otros recursos en la escuela o en la comunidad; usted puede ser un adulto con quien la gente joven puede conversar cuando necesita apoyo extra o un consejo; y usted puede dar a los estudiantes la información que pueda ayudarles a cuidarse bien a sí mismos y planificar para el futuro. Incluso si usted ve a muchos de los estudiantes sólo de vez en cuando, hay pasos que puede seguir para construir elementos fundamentales.

Aquí hay algunas ideas:

➤ **Ponga la lista de elementos fundamentales en su oficina o su área de trabajo.**

➤ Salude a los estudiantes cuando los vea—dentro o fuera de la escuela.

➤ **Use el lenguaje de los elementos fundamentales cuando hable con estudiantes, padres u otro personal.**

➤ Use el modelo de los elementos fundamentales como parte de cualquier evaluación y meta que usted establezca con los jóvenes.

➤ **Cuando hable con los padres, asegúrese de decirles qué es lo que a usted le gusta sobre sus hijos(as).**

➤ Cuando esté lidiando con estudiantes que están batallando, incluya cuantos elogios sinceros sean posibles dentro de la conversación (aunque sea sólo uno).

➤ **Si su comunidad tiene una iniciativa para construir elementos fundamentales, involúcrese.**

➤ Construya sus propios elementos fundamentales; usted estará mejor capacitado para tratar con sus estudiantes si usted se cuida a sí mismo.

➤ **Agradezca a los estudiantes cuando los vea construyendo elementos fundamentales para sus compañeros.**

➤ Ayude a coordinar noches de información y orientación para ayudar a que los padres y estudiantes localicen su salón de clase, conozcan al personal, aprendan sobre los servicios que usted proporciona y hagan preguntas antes de que la escuela empiece en el otoño.

➤ **Empiece un programa de ayuda a compañeros. Por ejemplo, ofrezca a los nuevos estudiantes grupos de apoyo que les ayuden a ajustarse en su nuevo ambiente escolar. Aquellos que se gradúen del grupo pueden liderarlo al año siguiente.**

➤ Ofrezca programas para asistir a los estudiantes que reflejen un enfoque en la formación de elementos fundamentales. Por ejemplo, cuando trabaje con la recuperación de estudiantes químico-dependientes, enfóquese tanto en los planes futuros y en las metas como en mantenerse sobrios.

➤ **Involucre a los estudiantes en entrevistas de fortalecimiento mientras procesan desafíos en sus vidas. Haga preguntas tales como: ¿Quién te protege? ¿Qué te protege? ¿Con cuáles recursos internos cuentas para recurrir cuando sea necesario? ¿Con quién puedes contar cuando necesites de apoyo extra?**

➤ Sea usted como un enlace entre las estaciones de radio y televisión locales para compartir con su comunidad las buenas noticias sobre su escuela.

➤ **Cuando hable de estudiantes específicos con otra persona del personal, enfóquese tanto en sus fortalezas personales como en sus desafíos. Si usted cree en los estudiantes, otros empezarán a creer en ellos también.**

➤ Trabaje con los maestros para incorporar la evaluación y el desarrollo de los elementos fundamentales dentro de las actividades en grupo y guiadas en el salón de clase. Por ejemplo, una unidad sobre carreras profesionales podría incluir una entrevista en la que los estudiantes hablen sobre cuáles elementos fundamentales ellos piensan que necesitan para tener éxito en el trabajo.

Ideas para educadores en organizaciones basadas en la fe para construir elementos fundamentales

Es muy posible que una de las razones por las que usted se comprometió a enseñar clases de educación basadas en la fe es que usted se preocupa muchísimo por la gente joven y quiere que prospere. Su compromiso hacia la gente joven y su participación en su vida pueden tener un gran impacto en sus Elementos Fundamentales del Desarrollo así como también en su crecimiento espiritual.

Aquí hay algunas cosas que usted puede hacer para ayudarles a construir sus elementos fundamentales:

➤ **Demuéstrele a cada joven en su clase o grupo que usted se interesa por él o ella. Salude a cada uno de ellos personalmente. Haga notar cuando ellos estén ausentes. Dígales "hola" fuera de las horas de educación religiosa.**

➤ Forme un ambiente en el cual las opiniones y experiencias de la gente joven sean valoradas y respetadas.

➤ **Deje que los niños(as) y jóvenes ayuden a escoger o adaptar el currículo que usted usa.**

➤ Enlace el aprendizaje en el salón de clase con el servicio a otros. Haga que su clase juegue con o lea libros a niños(as) en el jardín infantil o guardería. Haga que su clase prepare o enseñe una lección a niños(as) menores acerca de la solución pacífica de conflictos.

➤ **Sea bien claro sobre cómo usted espera que la gente joven se comporte en su clase o grupo. Fije reglas claras y justas y hágalas cumplir. Enseñe a la gente joven los límites de comportamiento que son una parte integral de la vida de una persona creyente en la tradición de su fe.**

➤ Desarrolle actividades significativas para la gente joven que les ayuden a ampliar su crecimiento personal, no solamente para ocupar el tiempo que tienen juntos. Puede empezar por involucrarlos en planificación y liderazgo.

➤ **Haga las lecciones interesantes, cautivadoras y relevantes a la vida de la gente joven. Sea creativo no solamente en el contenido sino que también en la estructura. Haga algunas actividades manuales o juegos que les enseñen y les diviertan. Llévelos a paseos cortos durante el tiempo que pasan juntos.**

➤ Dé a la gente joven las oportunidades de aprender, poner en práctica y enseñar la capacidad social. Haga representaciones sobre diferentes maneras para responder a ciertas situaciones. Enlace un pasaje de un texto sagrado a un elemento fundamental especifico de la capacidad social, tal como el elemento fundamental 33: capacidad interpersonal, que se refiere a la amistad y el tratar bien a los demás.

➤ **Asista a la gente joven a desarrollar su propia identidad ayudándoles a reconocer su fe internamente y a descubrir su propio sentido de propósito.**

➤ Encuentre a otros maestros que estén interesados en construir elementos fundamentales. Reúnanse con regularidad para compartir ideas, para discutir problemas y posibilidades y para celebrar lo que está funcionando en el salón de clase.

➤ **Fomente su propio desarrollo como maestro y como persona de fe. Construya sobre las fortalezas de los elementos fundamentales que usted posee.**

The List of Developmental Assets in French

Handout 90

40 Acquis dont les jeunes
ont besoin pour réussir (12 à 18 ans)

L e Search Institute a défini les pierres angulaires suivantes qui aident les jeunes à devenir des personnes saines, bienveillantes et responsables.

CATÉGORIE	NOM DE L'ACQUIS ET DÉFINITION
Soutien	1. **Soutien familial**—La vie familiale est caractérisée par un degré élevé d'amour et de soutien. 2. **Communication familiale positive**—Le jeune et ses parents communiquent positivement, et le jeune est disposé à leur demander conseil. 3. **Relations avec d'autres adultes**—Le jeune bénéficie de l'appui d'au moins trois adultes autres que ses parents. 4. **Voisinage bienveillant**—Le jeune a des voisins bienveillants. 5. **Milieu scolaire bienveillant**—L'école fournit au jeune un milieu bienveillant et encourageant. 6. **Engagement des parents dans les activités scolaires**—Les parents aident activement le jeune à réussir à l'école.
Prise en Charge	7. **Valorisation des jeunes par la communauté**—Le jeune perçoit que les adultes dans la communauté accordent de l'importance aux jeunes. 8. **Rôle des jeunes en tant que ressources**—Le jeune se voit confier des rôles utiles dans la communauté. 9. **Service à son prochain**—Le jeune consacre à sa communauté au moins une heure par semaine. 10. **Sécurité**—Le jeune se sent en sécurité à la maison, à l'école et dans le quartier.
Limites et Attentes	11. **Limites dans la famille**—La famille a des règlements clairs accompagnés de conséquences, et elle surveille les comportements du jeune. 12. **Limite à l'école**—L'école a des règlements clairs accompagnés de conséquences. 13. **Limites dans le quartier**—Les voisins assument la responsabilité de surveiller les comportements du jeune. 14. **Adultes servant de modèles**—Les parents et d'autres adultes dans l'entourage du jeune affichent un comportement positif et responsable. 15. **Influence positive des pairs**—Les meilleurs amis du jeune affichent un comportement responsable. 16. **Attentes élevées**—Les parents et les professeurs du jeune l'encouragent à réussir.
Utilisation Constructive du Temps	17. **Activités créatives**—Le jeune consacre au moins trois heures par semaine à suivre des cours de musique, de théâtre ou autres, et à mettre ses nouvelles connaissances en pratique. 18. **Programmes jeunesse**—Le jeune consacre au moins trois heures par semaine à des activités sportives, des clubs ou des associations à l'école et/ou dans la communauté. 19. **Communauté religieuse**—Le jeune consacre au moins trois heures par semaine à des activités dans une institution religieuse. 20. **Temps à la maison**—Le jeune sort avec des amis sans but particulier deux ou trois soirs par semaine.

ACQUIS EXTERNES

CATÉGORIE	NOM DE L'ACQUIS ET DÉFINITION
Engagement Envers l'Apprentissage	**21. Encouragement à la réussite**—Le jeune est encouragé à réussir à l'école. **22. Engagement à l'école**—Le jeune s'engage activement à apprendre. **23. Devoirs**—Le jeune consacre au moins une heure par jour à ses devoirs. **24. Appartenance à l'école**—Le jeune se préoccupe de son école. **25. Plaisir de lire**—Le jeune lit pour son plaisir au moins trois heures par semaine.
Valeurs Positives	**26. Bienveillance**—Le jeune estime qu'il est très important d'aider les autres. **27. Égalité et justice sociale**—Le jeune accorde beaucoup d'attention à la promotion de l'égalité, et à la réduction de la faim et de la pauvreté. **28. Intégrité**—Le jeune agit selon ses convictions et défend ses croyances. **29. Honnêteté**—Le jeune « dit la vérité même si ce n'est pas facile ». **30. Responsabilité**—Le jeune accepte et assume ses propres responsabilités. **31. Abstinence**—Le jeune croit qu'il est important d'éviter d'être sexuellement actif et de consommer de l'alcool ou d'autres drogues.
Compétences Sociales	**32. Planification et prise de décisions**—Le jeune sait comment planifier à l'avance et faire des choix. **33. Aptitudes interpersonnelles**—Le jeune fait preuve d'empathie et de sensibilité, et noue des amitiés. **34. Aptitudes culturelles**—Le jeune connaît des personnes d'autres cultures, races et ethnies, et se sent à l'aise avec elles. **35. Résistance**—Le jeune est capable de résister à des pressions négatives exercées par ses pairs et à des situations dangereuses. **36. Résolution pacifique de conflits**—Le jeune tente de résoudre les conflits sans recourir à la violence.
Identité Positive	**37. Pouvoir personnel**—Le jeune sent qu'il a le contrôle sur les choses qui lui arrivent. **38. Estime de soi**—Le jeune affirme avoir un degré élevé d'estime de soi. **39. Sentiment d'utilité**—Le jeune croit que sa vie a un sens. **40. Vision positive de l'avenir**—Le jeune est optimiste quant à son avenir personnel.

*(Catégorie générale à gauche : **ACQUIS INTERNES**)*

FEB 2 8 2013